THE INTERVIEW COACH

Hilton Catt and Patricia Scudamore

The Teach Yourself series has been trusted around the world for over 60 years. It has helped millions of people to improve their skills and achieve their goals. This new 'Coach' series of business books is created especially for people who want to focus proactively on a specific workplace skill and to get a clear result at the end of it. Whereas many business books help you talk the talk, the Coach will help you walk the walk.

THE INTERVIEW COACH

Hilton Catt and Patricia Scudamore

CONTENTS

MEET THE COACHES

Patricia Scudamore and **Hilton Catt** have 35 years' combined experience of interviewing and preparing candidates. Between them they bring the perspective of both recruiter and interviewee. From backgrounds in HR management, they set up their own business in 1988 and began writing on careers subjects 15 years ago. They have now written more than 20 books based on their experience of what it takes to make careers work in today's rapidly changing and uncertain world.

Patricia and Hilton were among the first to embrace the idea of people taking on the job of managing their own careers as opposed to leaving it to employers to do the thinking for them. They have seen for themselves the richness and diversity modern careers can offer and exploiting this richness and diversity to the full is one of the recurring themes in their work. They view writing books as the best way to spread their messages to the greatest number of people. Their other books in the Teach Yourself series include *Successful Career Change In A Week* (2013), *Successful Cover Letters In A Week* (2013) and *Successful Job Applications In A Week* (2012).

HOW TO USE THIS BOOK

✔ OUTCOMES FROM THIS INTRODUCTION

- Understand that interviews come in all shapes and sizes and are inherently unpredictable.
- Start to think about your attitude towards interviews by putting your current interview skills to the test in your first 'coaching session' – a simple questionnaire.

How good you are at interviews plays an important part in determining how successful you are going to be in life. Landing the right jobs means you get on and go places. Being turned down means you don't. It is little surprise, therefore, that the subject of interviews and how to be better at them always attracts a huge level of interest and may explain why you picked up this book in the first place.

THE EXPERIENCE YOU BRING WITH YOU

Unless you happen to be a complete newcomer to the world of work, you will already have some experience of applying for jobs and going to interviews. How much will depend on how active you have been on the job scene during the course of your career. For example, if you've applied for one job in your life, which happens to be the job you're in now, then your experience will be confined to an interview or interviews where the outcome for you was the one you wanted – that is, an experience that could hardly be described as typical. If, on the other hand, you've had to move jobs several times – and not always out of choice – then you will probably have seen a more representative sample of what's out there and the diversity of it all. Even better, you may have conducted some interviews yourself as part of your job. From this experience you will have seen how other people handle interviews: what impressed you and what didn't.

DIVERSITY AND THE CHALLENGE IT POSES

The first important observation to make about interviews is that they are diverse. Every one of them will be different; they conform to no standard patterns. The same is also true of interviewers. While some interviews are formal and structured, others are not. Likewise, some interviewers are experienced and professional, whereas others don't seem to have a clue about what they're doing. What this means in practice is that, when you're invited for an interview, it's hard to know exactly what to expect and how to prepare. Will you be put through a two-hour grilling or will you be in and out in 20 minutes – during which time the interviewer will be doing most of the talking?

The diversity of interviews and interviewers' styles poses a challenge for all job seekers. For example, an interview where the interviewer didn't ask you too many taxing questions may, on the face of it, mean that you got off lightly. At the same time, it could also mean that you didn't say all you wanted to say about yourself and some of your best points didn't come across. Good interviewers ask taxing questions to draw out information, so being put through the mill at an interview isn't necessarily a bad sign.

THE ENDURING POPULARITY OF INTERVIEWS

Despite the availability of a wide range of selection tests, interviews still remain the most popular method of assessing people's suitability for jobs. The chances of you being offered a job without having an interview are extremely remote. The only circumstances in which you might not have one are where an employer has previous knowledge of you. For example, you worked for the employer before or, increasingly likely these days, you have done time in the organization as a temp.

THE LIMITATIONS OF INTERVIEWS

Interviews don't, however, come without their problems. First and foremost is the fact that they rely on the skill and judgement of the people conducting them. Here it doesn't necessarily follow that interviewers know any more about interviewing than you do. Subjectivity is another issue. Even the most experienced interviewers find it hard to put their personal likes and dislikes to one side.

Given these inbuilt flaws, it is perhaps not surprising to see how many times interviewers get it wrong. The wrong person ends up getting the job – which is not good, of course, if that person happens to be you. The result would be that you find yourself in a job where you're out of your depth or where there are hidden snags that no one thought to tell you about. It may well be the interviewer's fault – but you're the one who ends up having to deal with the fall-out.

The message? Being good at interviews isn't just a case of knowing smart answers to questions. There is a lot more to it. For example, you also need to be able to:

- spot when interviews haven't covered all they need to cover
- take corrective action where necessary
- know what form the corrective action should take.

THE PURPOSE OF INTERVIEWS

Pause here for a few moments to ask yourself what your understanding is of the purpose of interviews. This isn't a trick question. In much of what has been written about interviews, the emphasis is usually placed on what employers seek to get out of them. There is, however, another party to consider and it is you, the candidate for the job, who has just as big a stake in the proceedings. You will want to know, for example, more about the job than the ad on the website told you. You will want to find out whether these are people you would get on with and enjoy working for. You will probably have a whole host of questions you will want answers to before you know whether the job is going to be right for you or not.

So, yes, interviews are where employers are looking at you as a prospective employee but, at the same time, you are looking at them as a prospective employer. It's a two-way process, and at the start neither the employer nor you knows how it will finish up. For example, what can happen during the course of an interview is that you find out something about the job that isn't to your liking. What this could mean is that you're no longer interested in it and, as far as your application is concerned, all you want to do is pull out as quickly as you can.

> ## ! COACH'S TIP
>
> ### Ask questions
>
> Sometimes it's you – not the interviewer – who needs to be asking the tough questions.

WHAT'S IN IT FOR *YOU*?

Two questions will be figuring in your thoughts as you pick up this book and start to read it:

1. Am I going to learn anything new?

2. How will this knowledge benefit me?

The book is a mixture of interactive exercises ('coaching sessions') and commentary text. The exercises are not just there to make you think. The idea is to involve you in the process of acquiring a better understanding of the subject matter by relating it to your own thoughts and experiences.

Each chapter has the following features:

✔ OUTCOMES FROM THIS CHAPTER

A bullet list at the start of each chapter sets out exactly what you will have got from that chapter by the time you have finished it. This is in terms of both what you will have *learned* (e.g. from the running text) and what you will have *done* (e.g. in the 'coaching sessions').

💬 COACHING SESSIONS

These are the key, meaty features within each chapter that will get you really working on, and interacting with, the ideas given in the commentary text. They include self-assessments, checklists and reflective questions.

❗ COACH'S TIPS

These are key, 'snappy' pieces of advice, often drawn from our own experience.

➡ NEXT STEPS

This section is an end-of-chapter bullet list summarizing what you have learned and placing that learning in the context of the chapters that follow.

👍 TAKEAWAYS

Reflective questions at the end of each chapter will help you focus on how what you have read and done in that chapter has helped you, *personally*.

In places as you read the book, you will come across information on how to access free downloads on subjects that may interest you.

At the end of the book you will find a 'help desk', which features answers to some of the questions people ask about interviews. There is also an action plan for you to make a note of any actions you plan to take. Finally, there is a summary sheet containing the key points from the book, to use as a quick aide-memoire.

What counts at the end of the day, after all, is what *you* get out of the book, what you take away with you when you've finished reading it, and how much of what you've learned is information you can use.

With this in mind, the book approaches the subject of interviews at a practical rather than a clinical level. The situations described are those that happen in real life and ones that you may have experienced yourself at some point. Similarly, the conundrums and tricky decisions described are those that people frequently have to face when they go for interviews and, unless you've done so already, ones you may have to face yourself one day.

THE AIM OF AN INTERVIEW

From your point of view, the aim of an interview is to present yourself to an employer in a way that accurately reflects:

- who you are
- what you can do.

If you manage to achieve this aim, employers will be able to see for themselves whether you're the right person for the job. If you don't, then you expose yourself to two dangers:

- You oversell yourself and find yourself in a job you can't hold down
- You do the opposite and find that you're rejected for jobs you could do with your eyes closed.

You're not everyone's sort

Going back to subjectivity, you won't hit it off with every interviewer you meet. Some will take a liking to you but some won't, in exactly the same way that you get on with some people you encounter in life but not others. You can go to an interview, make a good job of presenting yourself but still come away with nothing to show for it.

🗣️🗣️ COACHING SESSION 1

Put your interview skills to the test

Consider each of the following ten interview situations in turn and put a tick alongside the course of action closest to the one you would choose. Alternatively, use option F to write in your own answer.

You can look at the list again when you have finished reading the book. It will help you to see where and how your ideas may have changed.

1. You are invited to an interview in another part of the country. However, the letter you receive makes no mention of travelling expenses and this concerns you because you're out of work and short of funds. What's more, even if you go to the interview, there's no guarantee you're going to get the job. What do you do?

   A Decline the interview in case it's an expensive wild-goose chase ☐

   B Ask about travelling expenses when you get there ☐

   C Phone up first ☐

   D Wait and see whether you're turned down for the job then put in your bill for the money you've spent ☐

   E Say nothing and hope the interviewer will raise the subject of travelling expenses without you having to ask ☐

   F _____

   _____

   _____

2. You're running five minutes late for an interview and the traffic ahead grinds to a standstill. What do you do?

   A Feel you've blown it, turn round and go back home ☐

   B Phone in immediately and explain the situation ☐

   C Arrive late and hope your apologies will be accepted ☐

   D Get there as quickly as you can and hope that your latecoming won't be noticed ☐

   E Go back home and ring in next day to apologize when you're feeling more composed ☐

   F _____

   _____

   _____

3. You're told at the end of an interview that you stand a good chance of being put on the shortlist. A few days later, however, you receive a standard turn-down letter. What do you do?

A Phone in immediately and ask whether there's been a mistake ☐

B Nothing ☐

C Write in to ask why you were not put on the shortlist ☐

D Write in expressing your disappointment but at the same time making it clear that you would still be interested in the position if it ever became vacant again ☐

E Cross the company off your list of prospective employers ☐

F _____

_____

_____

4. An interviewer gives you no opportunity to ask questions about the job you're applying for – in fact, he seems to be in a hurry to bring the interview to a close. What do you do?

A Explain that you have some questions and ask whether it would be appropriate to go through them now or on another occasion ☐

B Say nothing and hope that another occasion will present itself ☐

C Send in your list of questions after the interview ☐

D Feel this is a reflection of the company's poor standards and write a letter afterwards withdrawing your application ☐

E Leave the list of questions until after you've been offered the job ☐

F _____

_____

_____

5. You arrive for an interview in a smart suit, only to find that the interviewer is wearing jeans, a casual shirt and trainers. What do you do?

A Apologize for overdressing ☐

B Take the interviewer's dress as evidence of the firm's poor standards and write in afterwards withdrawing your application ☐

C Ask for clarification of the company's dress code ☐

D Take off your coat in the hope that it will make you look more casual ☐

E Ignore the difference in your dress styles and carry on with the interview as normal ☐

F _____

_____

_____

6. An interviewer asks you a number of questions about your personal life that seem to have no relevance to the job. What do you do?

A Refuse point blank to answer the questions ☐

B Ask for the reasons for the questions before answering them ☐

C Walk out ☐

D Answer the questions as best you can ☐

E Wait to see whether you're turned down, then write a letter of complaint to the Chief Executive ☐

F _____

_____

_____

7. You're invited for an interview but you learn that you're one of 40 candidates. What do you do?

A Withdraw your application because you feel your chances of being shortlisted are slim ☐

B Attend ☐

C Phone up first and ask the company for an assessment of your chances ☐

D Say that you won't attend unless you can be guaranteed a place on the shortlist ☐

E As A, but giving your reasons, leaving it to the employer to persuade you to change your mind ☐

F _____

_____

_____

8. After an unsatisfactory interview in which the interviewer spent most of the time dealing with incoming telephone calls, you receive a letter telling you that you haven't been successful. What do you do?

A Appeal to the interviewer to reconsider the decision ☐

B Ask for another interview at a time when there will be fewer interruptions ☐

C Find out the name of the interviewer's boss and send a letter of complaint ☐

D Put it down to experience ☐

E Claim compensation for the waste of your time ☐

F _____

_____

_____

9. As an interview draws to a close, you realize that the interviewer has failed to touch on an important part of your experience – one highly relevant to the job under discussion. What do you do?

A Jump in immediately and point out the aspect of your experience that has seemingly been missed

B Say nothing in case it sounds as if you are being critical

C Write in after the interview

D Wait to see whether you're turned down and then write in

E Think that the interviewer has done a bad job and leave it at that

F _____

_____

_____

10. You arrive on time for an interview but the receptionist tells you that the interviewer is running over an hour late. What do you do?

A Sit down and wait

B Suggest to the receptionist that you can come back in 45 minutes and then, if this is acceptable, find somewhere comfortable nearby where you can sit down and have a hot drink

C Say an hour's too long to wait but that you'll ring the next day to make another appointment

D Tell the receptionist what the company can do with its job

E Take the view that a company that keeps interviewees waiting for an hour is not a company you would want to work for

F _____

_____

_____

→ NEXT STEPS

In this introduction you have:

- learned that interviews and interviewers are diverse

- grasped that an interviewer is not just about your prospective employer's needs, but yours, too

- learned the importance of asking questions

- assessed your own attitudes towards interviews.

In Chapter 1 we will be focusing on your role in the interview – the image you portray and making a good impression.

👍 TAKEAWAY

For this introductory 'takeaway' we would like you to explore your existing attitudes towards interviews, so that, as you work your way through this book, you will have a record against which to judge how your ideas are changing and developing.

Describe, broadly, your attitude towards interviews – do you see them as an opportunity to be embraced or as a hurdle to be overcome?

_____

_____

_____

_____

_____

_____

Describe your emotional response to interviews. Do you relish the thought of presenting yourself in the best possible light and putting across your message effectively, or do they fill you with trepidation and anxiety?

_____

_____

_____

_____

_____

_____

What has been your personal experience of interviews?

_____

_____

_____

_____

_____

_____

Do do you think interviews are still a useful tool?

_____

_____

_____

_____

_____

What do you think is the role of the interviewer?

_____

_____

_____

_____

_____

What do you think is the role of the interviewee?

_____

_____

_____

_____

_____

1 THE POWER OF YOU

✔ OUTCOMES FROM THIS CHAPTER

■ Understand the importance of being yourself when you go to an interview.

■ Know how to be better at engaging with employers.

■ See the value of making a good first impression.

■ Examine the quality of the image you present to people you've never met before.

■ Understand the importance of credibility.

ROUND PEGS FOR ROUND HOLES

When they interview people for jobs, employers are looking for someone who will be able to:

■ do the job

■ fit in with the team or situation.

Conversely, what they *don't* want is someone who is going to be out of their depth or a misfit. It comes down to finding round pegs for round holes and, ultimately, this is what selection is all about.

One of the big challenges interviewers face is finding out whether the people sitting in front of them are what and who they say they are, or whether they're putting on an act in an effort to impress them.

COACHING SESSION 2

Will the real you please step forward?

'Going to interviews is about looking good, having the right answers to questions and doing the best you can to make a favourable impression on the person sitting on the other side of the desk.'

Do you agree or disagree with this statement? Alternatively, do you think there is more to it than that?

Record your thoughts here.

_____

_____

_____

_____

_____

_____

_____

_____

WHY IT'S IMPORTANT TO BE YOURSELF

What most experienced interviewers will tell you is that people who try to impress by presenting themselves as someone they are not usually come unstuck. Keeping up an act for any length of time is hard, to say the least, and few people can do it with conviction. More often than not, they come across as cardboard cut-outs and interviewers feel that they have not connected with the real person. More to the point, how can an interviewer feel comfortable with someone who seems to be concealing their true personality? What are they hiding, and why?

The explanation for this behaviour is that it is often no more than an innocent wish to go to an interview and present an image which (mistakenly perhaps) candidates feel will come across more positively than the rather less glossy image that is the reality. Employers, however, have a natural tendency to back off from candidates who come across as false. They play safe. They offer the job to someone else.

COACHING SESSION 3

Are you for real?

Put yourself in an interviewer's shoes. How would you spot someone who is putting on an act? How would it affect your feelings about that person?

Record your thoughts here.

_____

_____

_____

_____

_____

_____

_____

_____

_____

_____

_____

There is a lesson here for those who approach interviews by rehearsing clever answers to questions and putting into practice techniques that have come straight out of a book they have just read. If the result is that they come across as someone putting on an act, then the impression they will make on the person interviewing them will be the opposite to the one they intended.

MAKING THE MATCHES

Interviewers have got a job to do, which is to find the right people to fill vacant positions. If they do the job well then everyone is happy, but if for any reason they make a wrong choice, the fallout for both the employer and the candidate is potentially serious. No one needs any reminders that employers are usually quick to act when they find they've taken on somebody who isn't working out.

> **! COACH'S TIP**
>
> **Be yourself**
>
> If you go to an interview and you can be yourself, employers stand a chance of seeing whether you're the right person for the job or not. Employers are on the same mission as you, so help them make the right decision. It's as much in your interest as theirs.

ENGAGING WITH EMPLOYERS

Engagement is the process of striking up a relationship with an employer through the medium of the person who interviews you. Put another way, if you hit it off with the interviewer your chances of getting the job are off to a good start. However, in most cases, the interviewer is going to be not only someone you've never met before but also possibly someone very different from you in terms of their age group, ethnic origin or social background. The question is: how would you get on if you had to hold a conversation with a complete stranger who has nothing in common with you? How would you engage with them?

Adding the fact that many interviewers aren't used to interviewing, so they may find the interview every bit as daunting as you do, makes the process of engagement even more challenging.

THE ART OF CONVERSATION

In an age where people on trains no longer talk to one another and instead spend their journeys either listening to music, staring at the screens of laptops and tablets or sending text messages to their friends, the art of conversation has almost become obsolete. The knock-on effect is the difficulty many people experience when they have to talk to somebody who is interviewing them for a job.

Having proper conversations with as wide a range of people as possible is great practice for going to interviews. 'Proper' in this context means:

- listening and taking an interest in what others have to say
- talking to them in language that they understand.

This is what engaging with people is all about and, at the end of the day, interviewers are people just like everyone else.

♤♤ COACHING SESSION 4

Practise your conversational skills

See what you can do to practise your conversational skills on people outside your normal circle of family, friends and work colleagues. See how you get on when it comes to talking to people who are complete strangers, people who are older or younger than you, and people who don't share the same background or common interests.

Having done this, reflect on your own conversational skills. How would you assess your ability to engage with people from a diversity of backgrounds?

Write down your thoughts here.

_____

_____

_____

_____

_____

_____

_____

_____

_____

_____

_____

_____

_____

_____

A BREATH OF FRESH AIR

What you also need to consider is that interviewing a succession of candidates one after the other can be mind-numbing and, even with the most seasoned professional, it's not long before the faces all start to merge into one – a fact you may be able to confirm from your own experience of interviewing. By engaging with interviewers, what you are seeking to be is the candidate who is like a breath of fresh air, the candidate who stands out, the candidate they remember.

What does it take to be a breath of fresh air? Here are some tips.

■ **Talk with enthusiasm and conviction**

An interview is an opportunity to tell an employer why you want the job and why you think you can do it. What you must do at the same time, however, is deliver these messages in a way that demonstrates that you believe in them yourself – that is, you should talk with enthusiasm and conviction. Sound as though you mean it.

■ **Make it interesting**

Another point to consider is that the best way to make an interviewer sit up and listen is by talking about something interesting. Interesting in this context means interesting to the interviewer, which, in turn, means relevant to the job for which you're applying. Candidates who ramble on about nothing of significance quickly lose the interviewer's attention. They become one of the faces that will merge with all the rest.

■ **Look friendly**

Remember that interviewers always welcome a nice friendly smile. It breaks the ice immediately. It is an important part of the process of engaging. Make a point of smiling more as you go about your day-to-day business until you reach the point where smiling becomes a conditioned reflex and you don't have to think about it.

♀♀ COACHING SESSION 5

The power of a smile

The human face has a wonderful ability to communicate important messages, not least the ability to smile and communicate a message of warmth and friendship. The effect in most cases is immediate – smile at someone and they smile back. Now put it to the test. Try smiling at a few people and see what reaction you get.

THE VALUE OF A GOOD FIRST IMPRESSION

Is it true that most interviews are decided in the first few minutes? It's certainly true that it's important to get an interview off to a good start. For example, take the classic bad start to an interview, which is arriving late – a position from which you will find it difficult or impossible to recover. The impact you make in those first few minutes therefore has a tremendous bearing on what follows.

What is the halo effect?

In the context of interviews, the halo effect describes the tendency to see some good points in a candidate at the start of an interview and thereafter to ignore any flaws that arise. The halo effect can also work the other way round. Bad points register at the beginning and cloud more favourable impressions that surface later on.

! COACH'S TIP

First impressions stick

What the halo effect teaches us is that once first impressions are formed they're very hard to shift.

🗪 COACHING SESSION 6

The first few minutes

What, in your opinion, helps to create a good first impression when you go for an interview?

_____

_____

_____

_____

_____

_____

_____

_____

_____

_____

_____

THE IMPORTANCE OF INDIVIDUALITY

Interviewers are surrounded by a sea of 'sameness'. Most CVs they see look the same. Most candidates they come face to face with say the same kinds of things. This is therefore an opportunity for someone who can introduce a little bit of themselves into an interview to score. It is useful to remember that interviewers will often bring candidates back to mind by referring to something they wore – for example, the chap with the nice blue tie, the girl with the unusual earrings, etc.

Your individuality – what marks you out as different from the rest of humanity – is important and nowhere more so than at an interview. It is what interviewers can and do latch on to. The styles of clothes you choose, the colours you put together and the way you wear your hair are all part of your individuality, but what makes them special is that they have an immediate impact where it matters most – which is at the start of an interview. They are what the interviewer notices first – as soon as you walk through the door.

COACHING SESSION 7

That 'little bit of you'

Cast your mind back to your last interview and, if you can, remember what you wore. Was there anything that an interviewer might have noticed? Was there anything that was different from what all the other candidates were wearing?

_____

_____

_____

_____

_____

_____

_____

_____

_____

> **! COACH'S TIP**
>
> **Be a bit different**
>
> See what's different about you as something good and something that you can use to your advantage when you go to an interview. Don't strive to be another 'suit' like all the rest. That little bit of you is what wins hearts and minds.

CREDIBILITY AND CONSISTENCY

Most of what candidates have to say about themselves at interviews is taken on trust. Where, however, the interviewer is given cause for doubt, it could be a case of saying goodbye to any chances of getting the job. Credibility is therefore an important issue.

> **QQ COACHING SESSION 8**
>
> **Credibility gaps**
>
> Can you think of ways in which candidates may put dents in their credibility? Draw on your own experience of doing interviews, if you have any.
>
> **Record your thoughts here.**
>
> _____
>
> _____
>
> _____
>
> _____
>
> _____
>
> _____
>
> _____
>
> _____
>
> _____
>
> _____
>
> _____

Credibility and consistency go hand in hand. Everything you say needs to be consistent; otherwise an interviewer who knows nothing about you will lose trust and confidence in you. Your credibility will be sunk and effectively you will have passed the point of no return.

An example of an inconsistency is a candidate who gives one reason for leaving a job on their CV and then says something completely different at an interview. It may sound like a minor issue but often it takes just one slip like this to undermine a candidate's entire credibility. The key message here is to be careful about what you say at an interview and make sure that any information you give marries up with information you have given elsewhere – for example in:

- your CV
- your cover letter
- an online application
- other application forms you have completed, either for the employer or for a consultant or headhunter who has been involved in sourcing you
- anything you might have said at a previous interview
- social networking sites.

> **!** **COACH'S TIP**
>
> ### Check your social media
>
> People put a lot of information about themselves on the Internet, often without realizing that employers considering them for key positions will take a look. Where an image doesn't fit with the image being presented at an interview, employers quite naturally start to ask questions.

COMFORT FACTORS AND THE INVISIBLE JOB MARKET

If you've ever had the job of recruiting someone to work in your team, you will know the importance of getting it right and what happens when you get it wrong. Not only is there the disruption that a misfit can cause but there is also the cost of exiting a bad choice, which, in today's world, includes the cost of dealing with any resulting litigation. For this reason, employers have to feel comfortable about the people they take on, which in turn explains why comfort factors play a large part in determining the outcome of interviews. If candidates A and B are both equally well qualified but the employer feels more comfortable with candidate A, candidate A will get the job and candidate B will be turned down.

Comfort factors have had a great bearing on the growth of the invisible job market, where positions are filled in a variety of ways including networking and approach. Especially where the position to be filled is at a senior level and where square pegs in round holes could have a very damaging effect, good candidates who are known to employers or who have been recommended will stand head and shoulders above those who are complete strangers.

WHAT GOES ON BEHIND THE SCENES

Even if networking or approach played no part in getting you the interview and you just went through the normal channel of applying for a job you saw advertised, there is still the strong possibility that your application won't be allowed to go too far before someone decides to do a little checking up on you. Sometimes the checking up will involve a letter or a phone call to the referee whose name appears in your CV – in other words, someone you should be able to rely on to say the right things. However, what is increasingly likely, in a world where employers look for comfort, is that they start tapping into their own networks for a little character background.

What this illustrates is the increasingly important part played by people who know you in bringing job applications to successful conclusions. Once upon a time the secret to success was described, cynically perhaps, as 'It's who you know, not what you know.' Today it's truer to say, 'It's who you know and what they know about you.'

The impact you make on others in your day-to-day life therefore has an increasingly important part to play in your success as you climb higher and higher up the ladder – hence the term **lifelong interview.** Of course, if you're smart enough, you can pull the wool over someone's eyes in a couple of 45-to 60-minute interviews, you can even fluff your way through the selection tests, but you won't do the same with someone who has known you for the last ten years.

! COACH'S TIP

Project a consistent image

It's no longer good enough to think in terms of saving up your best side for interviews. To work for you, the image you project has got to be one you project all the time. The consistency and application called for are not easy to achieve, so you may need to work hard at this.

COACHING SESSION 9

The background check

Imagine that a firm of headhunters has been retained to source suitable candidates for a job you would very much like to get. Imagine that, before talking to you, the headhunters decide to research your background by phoning round people who know you professionally – for example, your boss in your last job.

1. What kind of feedback would they get?

2. Would the feedback be good, and in what way?

3. Would it be good enough to make them feel comfortable about putting your name forward to their client? If so, why, and if not, why not?

COACHING SESSION 10

Your lifelong interview

Can you make a better job of your lifelong interview? Here is a tick list of desirable qualities for you to go through. As you do so, pick out the areas where you think you can improve – areas you need to focus on in your day-to-day dealings with your bosses, colleagues and other people you come into contact with in the course of your work.

Qualities to project	✓ / ✕
You don't have 'off' days.	
You're never the first to dress down.	
You don't get drawn into office gossip and tittle-tattle.	
You don't run down your bosses and colleagues behind their backs.	
You don't blame others for your mistakes – if it's your fault, you own up to it.	
Most importantly, you learn to keep your flaws to yourself.	

Areas for improvement and how you will improve them:

_____

_____

_____

_____

_____

_____

_____

_____

_____

_____

_____

_____

_____

_____

_____

→ NEXT STEPS

What makes the difference when you go for an interview? The answer is you – and the quality of the image you project to people you've never met before.

This chapter has been about examining your image. In particular, you learned:

- why it's important to present yourself as you really are and not as someone you're pretending to be

- how you can make a better job of engaging with interviewers

- that being credible means not doing anything to give interviewers cause to put question marks against your character

- the importance of making a good first impression – one that will carry you forward and influence the outcome of the interview.

In today's world of jobs, you need to think in terms of making a favourable impact on everyone you meet in the course of your work, not just interviewers (your lifelong interview).

The next chapter deals with what you need to consider before you go out into the job market. It examines the pitfalls that could get in the way of your ambitions and how to deal with them.

👍 TAKEAWAYS

Could you be accused of putting on a false front when you go for an interview? How do you think you could make a better job of 'being yourself'?

_____

_____

_____

_____

_____

_____

_____

_____

_____

_____

How do you perform when it comes to holding a conversation with a complete stranger? What practice do you get in talking to people you don't know and who come from a range of different backgrounds? After reading this chapter, do you think you could do more to improve your conversational skills? Say in what ways.

_____

_____

_____

_____

_____

_____

_____

_____

_____

Are you a good listener? Do you take a *proper* interest in what other people have to say to you? Alternatively, do you think you could benefit from paying more attention to your listening skills? Jot down any ideas you have had.

_____

_____

_____

_____

_____

_____

_____

_____

What kind of first impression do you think you make on people who have never met you before? Has reading this chapter made you think there could be room for improvement? Make a note of any points for action that have occurred to you.

_____

_____

_____

_____

_____

_____

_____

_____

_____

_____

Having read this chapter, do you think you are doing anything that could put dents in your credibility? If you are, what have you identified and what do you plan to do about it?

_____

_____

_____

_____

_____

_____

_____

_____

_____

Is your lifelong interview up to scratch? Are you confident that, if asked, people who know you would put in a good word for you? As a result of reading this chapter, what plans do you have for paying greater attention to the image you project to people you come into contact with in the course of your work?

_____

_____

_____

_____

_____

_____

_____

_____

_____

_____

_____

_____

Taking on board the advice in this chapter, do you think you can do any more to project yourself as the face that interviewers will remember? Make a note of any points for action.

_____

_____

_____

_____

_____

_____

_____

_____

_____

_____

2

PUTTING YOURSELF ON THE MARKET

✔ OUTCOMES FROM THIS CHAPTER

- Know what you need to consider before you start applying for jobs.
- Realize that you need to treat the time you can take off work to go to interviews as (a) precious and (b) not to be squandered.
- Know how to avoid interviews that are time-wasters.
- Remove barriers that you might be putting in the way of employers who want to talk to you.
- Assess how you respond to employers' emails and phone calls.

BEING READY

Going out into the job market needs to be done with planning and forethought. Otherwise you will encounter pitfalls that will get in the way of fulfilling your ambitions.

👥👥 COACHING SESSION 11

Interview pitfalls

Go through the following statements and put a tick in the box alongside those that reflect the way you see yourself.

Statement	✓ / ✗
'I find it hard to get interviews. I write off for lots of jobs I see advertised but most of the time all I get back is a polite "Sorry but no thank you" letter. I want to know what I'm doing wrong.'	
'I get interviews but then find I get no further. I've come to the conclusion that I must be doing something wrong. I'd like to know what it is.'	

'I always come away from interviews feeling I could have done better.'	
'Interviewers never seem to give me enough time to say all I want to say about myself.'	
'I go for interviews, get offered jobs, and then find myself turning them down because I'm not certain.'	
'I need to know more about the right way to answer questions.'	
'I find interviews impossible to read. I think I've given a good performance only to be turned down.'	
'Most of the interviewers I've met don't have a clue. They don't know the right questions to ask, so how can anyone possibly give a good account of themselves?'	
'I'd like to know what interviewers are looking for. What's behind their questions? What are they hoping to see when a candidate walks through the door?'	

PLANNING AHEAD

Unless you happen to be unemployed or your hours of work give you free time during the day, applying for jobs and going for interviews will mean taking time off work. If getting time off work is a problem for you, you are left with some difficult decisions to make.

COACHING SESSION 12

Getting time off for interviews

Consider the following case study. It illustrates the problem of how to get time off work to attend interviews.

Case study: Scott

Scott works in sales for a company that leases equipment to the construction and civil engineering industries. He is 28, ambitious and looking for a job where he will be better paid.

Scott fires off four enquiries to his company's main competitors asking whether they have anything suitable for him. He encloses a copy of his CV and in his cover letter he makes great play of the success he has had in working on key accounts and bringing in new business.

Scott is delighted when he gets emails back from each of the companies he has written to, all inviting him to attend an interview. This, however, is where Scott's problems start. If he goes to the interviews, it will mean he will have to take four days off work and he has only two days' leave entitlement left.

Imagine you are in the same situation as Scott. What would you do? Write your answer here.

_____

_____

_____

_____

_____

_____

_____

_____

For the case study in Coaching session 12, did you come up with any of the following ideas for taking time off work for interviews?

- Throw a 'sickie' or use a stock excuse like having to go to the dentist or a distant aunt's funeral.

- See whether any of the employers would be prepared to do interviews at weekends or out of hours.

- Turn down some of the interviews.

What we are looking at here, of course, is a list of choices that aren't very appealing and that, in most cases, could create more problems than they solve.

Even if your conscience doesn't stop you, stock excuses and sickie days quickly start to wear thin. You're first duty – always – is to look after the job you've got. Don't, whatever you do, get yourself into hot water with your boss because of the amount of time you are taking off work.

Employers are not always receptive to the idea of doing interviews out of office hours. Some will, some won't, but it isn't something you should bank on.

Turning down interviews speaks for itself. You won't get jobs unless you go to interviews, so finding you can't get time off work begs the question: what was the point of applying in the first place?

! COACH'S TIP

Plan your leave to allow time off for interviews

Always keep back some leave when you are putting yourself on the job market. Remember at the same time that you will probably have to attend more than one interview if you want your applications to progress any further than the preliminary stages.

Was there anything else Scott could have done better? Was there any other way he could have avoided being over-faced with interviews?

Full marks if you spotted it. With speculative job applications (unsolicited mailshots), it is a good idea to send them out in small batches rather than release too many at the same time. Four applications wouldn't normally be seen as too many but perhaps what Scott failed to take into account was the level of interest his CV and cover letter would spark off in businesses that competed directly with his own. A sales high-flier working for a competitor is always going to be worth asking in for an interview.

There is more on speculative job applications in Chapter 8, 'Interviews you get by proactive sourcing'.

ΩΩ COACHING SESSION 13

The time-wasting interview

Now consider what happens to Scott in the next part of the case study.

Case study: Scott (continued)

Scott resolves the problem of having too many interviews to go to by picking out the two companies he would most want to work for and turning the others down.

At the first interview, everything goes well until the subject of pay comes up. Scott tells the interviewer what he is earning and what he hopes to earn in his next job. The interviewer, however, shakes her head and says that the best offer she can make is way below the figure he is quoting and little improvement on what he is earning now. Scott takes the view that there is little point in proceeding any further with the interview because his only reason for seeking to make a move is to earn more money. He explains this to the interviewer and, after thanking her for her time, takes his leave.

Do you have any thoughts on how Scott got himself into this situation and how he could have avoided it? Write your answer here.

_____

_____

_____

_____

_____

_____

_____

AVOIDING INTERVIEWS THAT ARE TIME-WASTERS

Apart from learning that his salary is more or less in line with what one of his employer's competitors is paying, Scott's interview was a complete waste of time – his time and the interviewer's. What's more, he has incurred the added disadvantage of giving away one of the two days' leave entitlement he had left. And if his second interview turns out to be as unproductive as his first, he will have lost all his time-off work time so, apart from 'throwing sickies' or making other stock excuses, or prevailing upon employers to see him out of hours, Scott will be left with nowhere to go – at least until he has got some of his leave entitlement back (which could mean not until the following year).

DECIDING WHAT YOU WANT TO ACHIEVE

In a nice tidy world, situations like the one Scott found himself in would never happen. The mismatch between his salary ambitions and what the company he had applied to could afford to pay would have come to light sooner and Scott would not have been invited to the interview or lost a day of his precious leave entitlement. The fact that he did demonstrates perhaps that the job market is far from being a nice tidy world. In fact, it could be described as the opposite, which is one of the reasons why leaving anything to chance is a mistake.

What is apparent from the case study is that the interviewer had no idea of Scott's pay aspirations until the interview. Where he went wrong therefore goes back to the design of his CV and cover letter. Somewhere in these two documents, he should have been flagging up:

- his reason for looking for another job (salary improvement)
- the level of offer he would need to make it worth while for him to move.

Given this information beforehand, the interviewer would have seen the mismatch for herself and saved everyone time by not going ahead with an interview. Instead, she could have simply sent a polite letter to Scott thanking him for his enquiry and stating that there was nothing suitable for him at that moment.

> **! COACH'S TIP**
>
> **See your time-off work time as precious**
>
> In your cover letter and CV, always make it clear to employers why you are looking for another job and what you are hoping to gain from the move (where you are coming from and what you are seeking to achieve). Don't waste time on interviews that are pointless.

These points don't just apply to people like Scott, who are looking for more money. If, for example, you are looking for a job that is the next step up on your career ladder (e.g. from manager to director), again you need to make this clear. Then, no one will misread your intentions and invite you to an interview for a position that for you is merely a sideways step.

EXAMINING YOUR MOTIVES

Moving jobs is a big decision and it should never be taken lightly. With interviews, the speed at which events can move may occasionally take you by surprise, so it's important to examine your commitment before you start firing off job applications. Once you are certain that it's the right course of action for you and it's at the right time, you will be:

- ready when the offer is put in your hand
- ready to say yes.

COACHING SESSION 14

An over-hasty job application

Here is another case study for you to consider. It illustrates how we can waste time as a result of a quite different set of circumstances.

Case study: Lorna

Lorna works for a business specializing in asbestos removal and environmental monitoring. She joined the company when she graduated 12 years ago. It is the only job she has ever had.

Lorna's boss, Mike, is giving her a hard time. Mike isn't normally a difficult person to work for but he is under pressure from the Chief Executive to resolve a number of customer service issues that have manifested themselves recently. The tensions in the office come to a head one morning and Lorna and Mike end up 'having words'.

When she gets home later on, Lorna is still feeling angry with Mike. Then her eyes happen to fall on a job ad in the local evening newspaper, placed by a company in the business of recycling waste products from the food industry. The ad is for someone with her background and qualifications and it sets Lorna thinking. What if she handed in her notice and left? How would Mike manage without her? He'd soon be sorry for picking on her.

With these thoughts going through her head, Lorna sends off an application for the job. Two days later, she receives an email asking her to attend an interview with one of the recycling company's directors. The interview goes well and, before she knows it, Lorna is being offered the job. Taken aback by the speed of events and not knowing what to say, Lorna asks for a few days to think it over.

However, as she drives away from the interview, Lorna finds she is starting to have doubts about moving on. Things are more or less back to normal with Mike, then there is the thought of how to say goodbye to familiar faces and, more worrying still, how she would get on in a world that is going to be completely strange to her.

After spending a weekend troubled by such thoughts, Lorna decides to play safe and turn the offer down.

What are your thoughts on this case study? Record your answers here. Say what you feel you can learn from Lorna's experience.

_____

_____

_____

_____

_____

_____

Lorna fired off a job application because of a minor tiff with her boss and no doubt she found it made her feel better. Getting an interview probably gave her even more of a buzz but when, unexpectedly, she was offered the job the reality of it all began to kick in. Finally, when it came to the time for making a decision, she got cold feet.

It is a guess but, in Lorna's case, she may have been the only decent qualified applicant for the job so the interview became just a matter of seeing whether she ticked all the other boxes. Businesses in a hurry to fill positions can act in this way.

BEING THERE TO TAKE THE CALLS

Most interviews are arranged over the phone, so an important way of getting interviews is making sure that you're there to take the calls. The following case study illustrates how interview lists are commonly decided.

CASE STUDY: XYZ COMPANY

Halfway into the seasonal peak, XYZ Company loses one of its area account executives to a competitor. In the short term – and to stall any loss of business until a suitable replacement can be found – Pippa, XYZ's Sales Manager, takes over the vacant territory herself. This, she realizes, can't be allowed to go on for long because of the conflicting demands on her time. In fact, getting the vacancy filled as quickly as possible is her only way of keeping the competition at bay as well as reducing her workload.

Pippa places several ads and receives just over 40 replies. She takes the bundle of applications home with her one evening, thinking that she'll have more chance of some peace and quiet within her own four walls.

She starts the task of drawing up an interview list by dividing the applicants into two piles: those who look interesting and those who don't. Having done this, she then goes through the interesting pile a second time, picking out eight candidates who, from an experience point of view, look particularly promising. These, she decides, are the ones she is going to see, so, with her diary at the ready, she proceeds to ring up each of them. By now it is 8.30 p.m.

All of Pippa's eight selected candidates have included their home phone numbers in their CVs. She manages to contact five of these straight away and to fix suitable times and dates for interviews. Of the remaining three, one is a number that rings out (no one answers) and the other two are constantly engaged.

Next, Pippa tries the mobile numbers of the candidates she hasn't managed to contact. She strikes lucky with one but the other two numbers go straight to voicemail. Pippa leaves messages asking for a call back, either to the phone number of her apartment or to her mobile. That evening she hears nothing further from either candidate and it is the same story the following morning.

Pippa considers her options. On the one hand, she already has six candidates booked in for interview but, on the other, she would still ideally like to see a couple more. Here she decides to go back to the candidates she originally picked out as 'interesting' (the ones she didn't put on the interview list). Flicking through them again, she finds two candidates who on second inspection look reasonable, so she rings them up using the mobile numbers they have given. In both cases, she manages to contact them straight away and interview times are fixed.

What about the two candidates she still hasn't heard from? Pippa takes the view that she has given them long enough to contact her, so, if they do surface at any point, she'll tell them tough luck. She feels that she can't wait indefinitely for people to return her calls. She's got more pressing priorities to think about.

You may not think much of Pippa's method of putting together an interview list, but it is typical of organizations where the job of sourcing suitable people falls on the shoulders of managers who don't have the luxury of time on their side. It's worth remembering these points:

- They use the phone to make contact with people.

- They ring when it suits them.

- The calls can come at any time (including evenings and weekends).

- They don't waste time on people who are hard to contact.

! COACH'S TIP

Increase your chances of getting an interview

The question almost all unsuccessful candidates ask is, 'Why didn't they ask to see me when I've got all the experience and qualifications to do the job blindfold?'

The answer in a lot of cases is a simple one. These are the people who weren't there to take the calls. The 'Dear John...' letter they received didn't tell them that, of course.

DOING AN AVAILABILITY AUDIT

The amount of communication gadgetry on the market has mushroomed in recent years, to the point where today there are no excuses for being hard to contact. Having said this, some people still are and sadly they pay the price in a world where competition for good jobs is intense and, like Pippa, employers usually have plenty of other candidates to fall back on.

Running through a checklist like the one below is a useful way of checking whether, without knowing it, you are putting barriers in the way of employers who may be trying to contact you. Known as an availability audit, it is intended to throw up points for action when you're applying for jobs, such as whether you need a facility for voicemail on your home phone or whether you simply need to be more diligent about checking messages.

COACHING SESSION 15

How easily can you be contacted?

How would a prospective employer get on if they needed to contact you in a hurry? Go through the following list of questions and put a tick alongside those to which you could truthfully answer yes.

Question	✓ / ✗
Would they have phone numbers and an email address on which they could contact you?	
If they needed to speak to you out of hours, would they have your home phone number and/or the number of your mobile?	
Are you sure it wouldn't be difficult for people to contact you out of hours, on phones that aren't answered or are engaged for long periods?	
Does your phone at home have a voicemail facility?	
If so, do you check your voicemail messages regularly?	
Is your mobile always switched on at times when employers might be trying to get hold of you?	
Do you check your mobile regularly for voicemail messages and missed calls?	
Do you need to introduce some discipline at home about how long people spend on the phone?	
Do you need a call-waiting bleep or some other facility on your phone to alert you when someone is trying to get through?	
Do you need to set up a link from your home phone to your mobile?	

Email addresses

Putting a personal email address in your CV and cover letters (as opposed to an office email address) is another way of enhancing your availability. It gives employers another way of contacting you quickly. It means that three routes are available to someone who wants to contact you in the evenings or at weekends: home phone, mobile phone and email. Email is only any good if you check your messages regularly (some people are less diligent when it comes to checking personal email accounts). An email would normally be a message asking you to ring the employer to arrange the interview. The important point here is to make sure that you do it quickly. Having the facility to access emails remotely (e.g. a smartphone) is an added advantage, particularly if your job means that you're frequently on the move.

Text messaging

Some employers use text messaging as a way of making contact with candidates. Like an email, a text message would normally be used to ask you to ring them. Again, when you're active on the job scene, make sure that you check your text messages regularly and act on them immediately.

> **! COACH'S TIP**
>
> ### Work on your availability
>
> In today's high-speed world, being there to take the calls is an essential part of the process of getting you to interviews. If you work on improving your availability, it will play to your advantage.

> **COACHING SESSION 16**
>
> ### Being 'employer friendly'
>
> It is important to see what employers' problems might be and do your best to remove any difficulties they have in contacting you. (There is more on being employer-friendly later.)
>
> List here three ways in which you could make life easier for employers who are trying to contact you.
>
> 1 _____
>
> _____
>
> 2 _____
>
> _____
>
> 3 _____
>
> _____

Contacts through third parties

Employers are not the only ones who use the phone to fix up interviews. A lot of recruitment is done through consultants, some of whom operate as employment agencies. Consultants are even less inclined to spend time on candidates who are difficult to contact. In many cases, they work on commission, which can be earned only by making successful placements. Candidates who don't return their calls or who take days to reply to email messages don't endear themselves to consultants.

BEING READY TO GO TO INTERVIEWS AT SHORT NOTICE

Interviewers often want to call in candidates at short notice, leaving them faced with the problem of getting the time off work. The difficulties are even greater where the candidates in question don't want it generally known that they're looking for another job and where they're trying to keep their job-hunting activities to themselves. Even taking a half-day holiday could be awkward when it has to be done at the drop of a hat.

💬💬 COACHING SESSION 17

The short-notice interview

Imagine you've applied for a job and you get a phone call asking you to attend an interview in two days' time. Imagine, however, that, on hearing this, your heart sinks because you realize that the date being suggested clashes with an arrangement you've already made to visit an important client. You explain your predicament to the caller who agrees the request is at short notice but explains that he is going on a fortnight's holiday the following week and he wants to get the interviews done before he goes.

How would you handle this situation? Give your thoughts here.

_____

_____

_____

_____

Positive thinking

An initial (and entirely understandable) reaction to being asked to attend an interview at short notice is to blame the interviewer for expecting too much and treading beyond the bounds of reasonableness. But pause for thought a moment. There are some decided advantages for you if you could find some way of seeing this interviewer before he disappears on his fortnight's holiday. Consider the following:

- Getting everything done and dusted quickly means you could have the offer of a job in your hands sooner than you hoped.

- Most importantly, unless they happen to be out of work, other candidates for the job will also be having trouble getting time off at short notice, to the point where some of them may have to say they can't. The upshot here is fewer candidates and less competition, which could mean a good outcome for you.

- By not allowing yourself to be swayed by negative thoughts, you might in fact be able to come up with ways of accommodating the request to interview you at short notice. For example, could you offer to see the interviewer after hours or when you get back from visiting your client? In these situations, don't leave it to interviewers to have all the bright ideas. Have some of your own up your sleeve.

COACHING SESSION 18

Preparing at short notice

Can you think up some ways in which you could be better prepared for interviewers who drop on you at short notice?

Give your answers here.

_____

_____

_____

_____

_____

_____

_____

_____

_____

HOLIDAYS AND INTERVIEWS

Short notice or not, holidays can get in the way of interviews, especially if you are away for periods of more than one week. For example, if you happen to be going off on a fortnight's holiday at the same time that an employer has pencilled in dates for a round of second interviews, then it will be a test of your powers of persuasion to see whether you can get everything put on hold until you get back. Some employers won't, however, be prepared to put everything on hold and you may be informed politely that it's your hard luck.

COACHING SESSION 19

Holiday planning

Can you think of ways of avoiding your interviews coming into conflict with your holidays?

Write your answers here.

_____

_____

_____

_____

_____

_____

_____

_____

_____

_____

_____

_____

_____

_____

_____

When asked, people can often come up with various ideas for organizing their holidays in more 'interview-friendly' ways. Here are four that might interest you – you can compare them with the answers you gave above.

When you're applying for jobs, take your holidays in periods of no more than one week at a time.

Choose your holiday destinations carefully – pick places from which you could get back if the need to attend an interview arose.

Suggest doing the interview via a webcam link.

Try to avoid sending off job applications in periods coming up to when you're due to take holidays.

Using voicemail

When employers phone you to arrange interviews, they should be able to speak to you or, if you're not there, be greeted by your voicemail message. Your voicemail message will either be the standard greeting provided by your phone service provider or a message you have recorded yourself because, quite rightly, you feel it is more personal and welcoming.

What you don't want, of course, is for your personal recording to come across as frosty or pompous or anything else that might put callers off. Voicemail messages have put paid to quite a few people's job-seeking and interview ambitions, though they'll never know it.

Some people even record silly messages, which may verge on the irritating and imbecilic. Worse still, a few might even be classified as offensive. No doubt the composers of these messages find them extremely funny (why else do they do it?) and probably intend them solely for the amusement of their friends and family.

The simple point here is this: make your voicemail message consistent with what you would be happy for a prospective employer to hear. If in doubt, wipe it out and rerecord it. The idea with a voicemail message is to sound friendly yet at the same time professional. You need to come across as someone people feel they can do business with. Ultimately, what you want is for the caller to leave a message and not to put the phone down.

COACHING SESSION 20

The right voicemail message

Listen to your voicemail message and, as you do so, put yourself in the position of an employer who is phoning you to fix up an interview. Try rerecording your voicemail message a few times and, better still, get someone else to give you a frank opinion on how you sound. Voicemail messages can be an important first impression, so it pays to make sure that the impression you give is the one you intend.

Use this space to draft your message.

_____

_____

_____

_____

_____

_____

_____

_____

_____

_____

_____

_____

_____

COACH'S TIP

Add more numbers to your voicemail

When you're active on the job market and putting out applications, add to your voicemail message alternative phone numbers that callers can reach you on, for example your mobile. This information will be in your cover letter and CV, of course, but there is no harm in repeating it. It is all part of being 'employer-friendly'.

BRUSHING UP YOUR TELEPHONE MANNER

As soon as your CV has gone out, there is the possibility that an employer will ring you at home to fix up an interview. However, family life can be intrusive and loud, and anyone who has had the job of phoning candidates at home will tell you how difficult it is to have an intelligent conversation with someone over a barrage of background noise – for example, a television turned up too loudly.

Good first impressions are at stake again, so here are three points to remember when taking that call.

1. When you answer the phone, do it in the way you would answer a call in the office, e.g. 'John Smith. Good evening.'

2. Instil the message about answering the phone in a proper way to anyone else at home who might pick up the call, for example members of your family.

3. Have a place earmarked where you can take the phone and hold a conversation with someone in reasonable peace and quiet.

! COACH'S TIP

Find somewhere quiet

When you are talking on the phone, background noise is distracting at the best of times. When you are taking an important call about a prospective interview, you will think better and find it easier to concentrate if you don't have to deal with such distractions, so make sure you can talk undisturbed.

→ NEXT STEPS

This chapter has been about the preliminary groundwork you need to do before you start applying for jobs – groundwork such as:

- making sure you can get the time off work
- seeing the time you take off work as precious
- not wasting time on interviews that are pointless.

In the business of applying for jobs, people tend to judge their performance by the number of interviews they succeed in getting. You don't get jobs unless you get interviews is the reasoning here, so the more the merrier. But if the jobs don't interest you even if they were to be offered to you, the interview count is meaningless. Yes, you want interviews, but only if they're the right ones.

What you need therefore is a way of filtering out those interviews that aren't going to go anywhere. The best way to do this is by using your cover letter and CV to make it plain to employers what it is you want to get out of your excursion into the job market. By doing this, you will have done all you can to prevent employers misreading you and inviting you to interviews for jobs which are entirely unsuitable. More money, a step up the ladder or perhaps just a job that can offer you more security – whatever it is you want, make it crystal clear. What's more, by doing this, you are helping employers to make the right decision – see the employer-friendliness as being as much in your interests as theirs.

Also in this chapter, you have seen how candidates who are hard to contact (for example candidates who don't return their voicemail messages or respond to their emails promptly) often miss out on interviews. Employers give up on them and move on to someone else. In today's world you have to engage the job market with what it wants, which is good candidates who are trouble-free to deal with. This is the point of being employer-friendly.

Having done the preliminary groundwork, you are now at the point where you are ready to start sending off applications. The next step will be to look at what, to many candidates, is the most bewildering aspect of interviews: their diversity and knowing what to expect when you are invited to one.

Linked to the diversity of interviews is the diversity of interviewers: at one extreme the well-groomed professional, at the other the novice who has never done an interview before and has less idea of how to go about it than you do.

- Is there a way of predicting the course an interview is going to take or is it a case of going along and being prepared for anything?
- How do you engage with interviewers who are clueless?
- How do you compensate for their lack of ability to put the right questions?
- In these situations, how do you steer the outcomes to the ones you want?

The next chapter deals with these issues.

👍 TAKEAWAYS

Are you doing enough to communicate your ambitions? Do you plan to make any changes to the design of your cover letters and CVs that will make it clearer to readers what you are seeking to gain from your next job move? What are the changes you are going to make?

_____

_____

_____

_____

_____

_____

_____

_____

_____

_____

Have you ever found yourself in an interview that is a complete waste of time? Make a note here of anything you plan to do to ensure that this doesn't happen again.

_____

_____

_____

_____

_____

_____

_____

_____

_____

Why are you looking for another job? Write down the reasons here. Are you satisfied that these reasons are strong enough to ensure that you won't have an attack of cold feet when the job is offered to you?

_____

_____

_____

_____

_____

_____

_____

_____

_____

Have you learned anything from this chapter about how you could plan your holidays in a way that will avoid conflict with interviews? Is there anything different you will be doing in future?

_____

_____

_____

_____

_____

_____

_____

_____

_____

_____

What more can you do to make it easier for employers to contact you? If you have come up with any points for action, write them down here as a reminder.

_____

_____

_____

_____

_____

_____

_____

_____

_____

_____

How would you get on if an employer asked you to attend an interview at short notice? What more can you do to accommodate employers who want to move quickly? Make a note of any ideas.

_____

_____

_____

_____

_____

_____

_____

_____

_____

_____

In the light of what you have read in this chapter, do you plan to make any changes to your voicemail greetings or the way you answer the phone? Write down what you plan to do.

_____

_____

_____

_____

_____

_____

_____

_____

_____

_____

_____

_____

_____

_____

HANDLING THE DIVERSITY OF INTERVIEWS

- Understand the difference between good and bad interviews.
- Understand different types of interview and what to expect.
- Plan strategies for interviews to take account of their diversity.
- Understand the importance of managing interviews and keeping control.
- Know how to spot where the problem could be you.

THE BAD INTERVIEW EXPERIENCE

Practically everyone who has been active on the job scene for several years will have chalked up at least one bad interview experience. Bad interview experiences range from candidates being kept waiting in cold draughty corridors for long periods, through to interviewers who spend most of the interview either taking incoming phone calls or talking about themselves.

Candidates who have had these bad experiences tend to feel that they have been short-changed – and who can blame them? The final insult for many is a curt letter a few days afterwards to say that they have been turned down for the job. What this proves, apart perhaps from the need for a skin as thick as a rhinoceros, is that in today's world of job-hunting, bad interview experiences are a fact of life. To be prepared for them is just a case of facing up to reality. To be put off by them is something you can't afford to let happen. (There is more on this subject in the final chapter of the book.)

Bad interview experiences have been on the increase in recent years, or so it seems. Is there a reason for this?

What won't have escaped anyone's attention is the tendency in organizations to place more and more work into fewer and fewer pairs of hands – all done for cost-cutting reasons, of course. People who are tasked with carrying out interviews are, in many cases, busy managers who have had no training and who have other conflicting demands on their time. Their approach is intuitive rather than structured and often the results are shambolic.

COACHING SESSION 21

Your thoughts about interviews and interviewers

Based on your experience of interviews and interviewers, do you agree or disagree with the following statements?

Statement	Agree/disagree
Most interviewers don't have a clue about what they're doing.	
Most interviewers don't ask the right questions.	
Interviewers make their minds up in the first five minutes.	
Interviewers don't allow enough time for their interviews.	
A bad interview is one where the interviewer does most of the talking.	

WHAT MAKES A GOOD INTERVIEWER?

Good interviewers are, first and foremost, good listeners. A good interview is therefore one where the candidate does most of the talking – at least up to the point where it is the candidate's turn to sit back and be told more about the job. A bad interview is conversely one where the candidate doesn't get a chance to say very much. The interviewer doesn't ask the right questions – typically asking those that call for only 'yes' or 'no' answers instead – or the interviewer interrupts every time the candidate starts to say anything.

COACHING SESSION 22

The too-talkative interviewer

What would you do if you found yourself in an interview where you want to say a great deal about yourself but the interviewer won't let you get a word in edgeways?

Write your ideas here.

_____

_____

_____

_____

_____

Fortunately, most interviewers are competent, so all you have to do is answer the questions they put to you, ensuring as you do so that the messages you want to impart are coming across.

DIFFERENT TYPES OF INTERVIEW

Rather like interviewers, interviews also come in all shapes and sizes. Most are conducted face to face but some are done remotely, either by phone or over the Internet. The number of people interviewing you can also vary, ranging from simple one-on-ones through to interviews conducted in front of panels. Broadly speaking, though, interviews divide into three main types:

1. Preliminary interviews

These are used to whittle down large numbers of candidates into a more manageable group for final selection purposes. Their purpose is to establish 'broad suitability' rather than to decide to whom to offer the job. A point to note about preliminary interviews is that they are often done in quick succession, with one candidate being seen straight after another. Interviewers will therefore be keen not to let their interviews overrun because, if they do, it will have a knock-on effect on the rest of the interviews that day. Preliminary interviews are the subject of Chapter 6.

2. Shortlist interviews

These occur once the preliminary interviews have taken place, when some of the candidates are put on a shortlist and asked to come back for a second showing. There could be more than one shortlist interview, reflecting either indecision ('Let's take a look at them all again') or a further whittling down (say from six to three). A shortlist interview will tend to last longer than a preliminary interview. The employer will be hoping to make a final selection this time, so more ground will need to be covered. Shortlist interviews are the subject of Chapter 7.

3. Interviews you proactively sourced

These come about as a result of tapping into the invisible or unadvertised job market and they are quite different from the first two types. This type of interview is dealt with in Chapter 8.

INTERVIEW STRATEGIES

The first point to make about the diversity of interviews is that, if you approach them all in the same way, you will come unstuck. To illustrate this, take a look at the following case study.

CASE STUDY: OLIVIA

Olivia, an architectural technician, is looking for another job because the practice where she works is closing its office locally and moving to another part of the country. Olivia does not want to relocate because it would mean her partner having to give up his job and the children moving to new schools.

Olivia sees a job advertised with a local company that designs and manufactures purpose-made cladding systems for landmark buildings. Olivia applies and soon receives a letter inviting her to attend a preliminary interview with the company's human resources manager.

Olivia is already acquainted with the company's products because they have featured in some of the projects she has worked on in her present job. Nevertheless, she does some further research into the company by visiting its website and looking at articles in various technical journals. She also puts together a portfolio of some of her better work. Then, as part of her preparations for the interview, she rehearses a presentation of the material in her portfolio.

On the day of the interview Olivia arrives early but she is kept waiting for 20 minutes because the interviews are running late. While she is waiting, two other candidates for the job arrive.

The interviewer, who introduces himself as Al, apologizes for the late start, whereupon Olivia asks him whether he would like to look at her portfolio. Olivia notices that Al seems to hesitate before saying yes but she decides not to let this put her off. She proceeds to deliver the presentation she has rehearsed, going though the material in her portfolio page by page.

After she has been talking for ten minutes Al interrupts her, saying that he needs to move on because he has other candidates waiting. This takes Olivia aback. Some of the more interesting projects are at the end of her portfolio and she hasn't reached them yet – she intended them as a grand finale. She tries to explain this to Al but he is already going through her CV and firing questions at her. His pace is brisk and, on two occasions, he cuts her answers short.

Finally, he asks Olivia whether there is anything she wants to know about the job. She asks what computer-aided design packages the company uses, to which Al replies that he doesn't know. Then, explaining he has someone else waiting, he brings the interview to a close. He tells Olivia that he will be in touch soon.

A week later Olivia gets a letter to say that she has been unsuccessful. Olivia views her experience as a bad interview with a bad interviewer – someone who didn't know anything about the job, someone who didn't give her a chance to bring out her best points.

🗪 COACHING SESSION 23

The failed interview

What are your thoughts about Olivia's experience? Was she to blame for what happened in any way? If so, where did she go wrong? Or was it all the interviewer's fault?

1. Write your thoughts here.

_____

_____

_____

_____

_____

_____

2. Faced with the same situation, what would you have done? Write your answer here.

_____

_____

_____

_____

_____

_____

_____

_____

Being concise and flexible

Pictures, portfolios and presentations do have a part to play in interviews (and you will be learning more about how to use them to good effect later in the book), but what Olivia's case study illustrates is that they are not always appropriate:

- You need to have strategies for interviews that take account of a diversity of possible scenarios – in Olivia's case, an interviewer who was running late with his interviews, struggling to catch up and failing at the same time.

- Any planning you do can work against you if what you plan is not concise, flexible or capable of being changed. In Olivia's case, she stuck doggedly to her plan to deliver her presentation and failed to pick up the warning signs that the clock was ticking against her.

COACHING SESSION 24

Working out what to expect

Is knowing what to expect in advance of an interview largely a guessing game? Use Olivia's case study to answer the following questions:

1. What in your opinion, could she have sensibly predicted about the interview with Al?

_____

_____

_____

2. What, on the other hand, was not predictable?

_____

_____

_____

3. Now give your reasons.

_____

_____

_____

_____

_____

_____

_____

Being prepared for the unexpected

Olivia had been told that the interview would be a preliminary interview with the company's HR manager. From this information she could have gathered that one of the major challenges she would face would be how to get her important messages across in an allotted period of time, and to a non-specialist.

In other words – and irrespective of any mismanagement on Al's part – she could have predicted that the clock would be ticking against her. The ability to be concise and flexible is particularly important in preliminary interviews, where the next candidate could already be waiting outside before you've had a chance to say all you want to say.

On the other hand, it would have been reasonable for Olivia to expect a better performance from Al. After all, he was a human resources manager and, as such, he should have known enough about conducting interviews to avoid getting into the situation he found himself in – a situation that worked to Olivia's detriment.

! COACH'S TIP

Be ready for anything

You can do the intelligent guesswork but you still need to be ready for anything. More to the point, you need to be tuned in to picking up signals when the interview:

- is going off course

- may require input from you to get it back to where it should be.

MANAGING INTERVIEWS AND KEEPING CONTROL

In a world of uncertain standards, another aspect of managing diversity concerns the need for you, the interviewee, to play an active rather than a passive role in determining the direction an interview takes.

COACHING SESSION 25

Playing an active role

The following case study illustrates what can happen if an interview discussion focuses on irrelevant matters.

Case study: Joe

Joe is sitting in a preliminary interview where the interviewer has spent over 15 minutes chatting about Joe's first job, a job he left ten years earlier. The interviewer, it turns out, once worked for the same company, so most of the questions Joe is being asked are about personalities who worked there rather than what he did, what experience he gained and why he left.

The interview is for a position where experience Joe gained more recently – in his present job – has more relevance as far as his suitability is concerned. Despite this, the interviewer is showing no signs of wanting to move on with Joe's employment history and Joe is already starting to pick up signals that the time is running out and the interview is about to be brought to a close.

What would you have done in Joe's position? Write your answer here.

_____

_____

_____

_____

_____

Pre-emptive strikes

Sometimes, towards the end of an interview, the interviewer will ask you whether you have anything you want to add, but it's best not to bank on this.

In Joe's case, the interview's descent into a friendly chat about old times could have been a sign that the interviewer had already formed a positive view of him: Joe ticked all the boxes as far as the test of broad suitability was concerned and he's on his way to the next stage. On the other hand, it could mean that the interviewer didn't make a good job of the interview by not covering important areas of Joe's experience (important to him) in the way they should have been.

Joe now has the choice of either saying nothing or taking the responsibility on himself for mentioning the experience he's had in his current position. The latter is known as a **pre-emptive strike** and it forms part of the important principle of **keeping control** over:

- the messages you need to impart
- how you deliver these messages.

The manner in which you do this is, of course, important. You want to be helpful. You're not trying to tell the interviewer how to do his or her job. You are always mindful of the fact that interviewing is a subjective process, so if the interviewer starts to feel hostile towards you there is a strong chance that your application will go no further. On the other hand, the interview could be your one and only opportunity of presenting your credentials for the job and it would be contrary to your best interests to let the opportunity slip by.

You will find more on pre-emptive strikes and keeping control throughout the book.

COACH'S TIP

Keep control of interviews

To make sure you deliver your important messages, be prepared to take action when interviewers don't ask the questions they need to ask. This may mean saying something along the lines of 'Oh, by the way, I thought I ought to mention...' as an interview draws to a close. Whatever you do, don't walk away from an interview feeling that you've not said everything you should have done. You may not get another chance.

→ NEXT STEPS

In this chapter you have been looking at the challenges posed by interviews that don't conform to standard patterns. You have seen how you need to make allowances for interviewers who aren't very good and how their shortcomings should never be allowed to get in the way of your chances of getting the job. If you're the best candidate, this has got to come across, irrespective of whether or not the interviewer asks the right questions or structures the interview in the right way.

You have learned that there are several ways to do this. In a world where you can't rely on interviewers to get it right every time, you need to keep a controlling hand on the process that is unfolding. Where you sense that the interviewer's agenda is confused, you may need to step in. For example, if you think one of your best qualifications for the job is being overlooked, you can, at the appropriate moment, draw it to the interviewer's attention.

Interviews are not a battleground, where you and the interviewer slug it out eyeball to eyeball to see who comes out of it scoring the most points. The interviewer and you have a shared interest. You don't want a job where you will be struggling and neither do employers want to hire people who are going to fail. Interviews are therefore a common meeting ground between two parties whose aims are the same.

The next chapter takes you on to the job of preparing for interviews: what to do when you get the invitation and, if you want the interview to go well, what you need to do before you go.

 **TAKEAWAYS**

Look at coaching session 21 again. Have any of your opinions about interviews and interviewers changed as a result of reading this chapter? If they have, say why.

_____

_____

_____

_____

_____

_____

_____

_____

_____

After reading this chapter, do you think you are any better equipped for dealing with bad interview experiences? Say in what way you feel better equipped.

_____

_____

_____

_____

_____

_____

_____

_____

_____

_____

_____

Has the case study of Olivia caused you to think where you may be going wrong with planning your strategy for interviews? What thoughts did you have? Record them here.

_____

_____

_____

_____

_____

_____

_____

_____

_____

To take account of the diversity of interviews, have you come up with any ideas on how you could make your approach more flexible and capable of change? Make a note of your ideas.

_____

_____

_____

_____

_____

_____

_____

_____

_____

_____

Is the message about 'being prepared for anything' one that is borne out by your own experience? Can you think of an example of where you were caught on the wrong foot at an interview? What did you learn from the experience? Do you have any thoughts on how you could avoid being caught out again?

_____

_____

_____

_____

_____

_____

_____

_____

From your own experience, can you think of an example of where the interviewer failed to ask you the right questions? At the time, what did you do to address the interviewer's omissions? After reading this chapter, would you handle the situation any differently?

_____

_____

_____

_____

_____

_____

_____

_____

_____

_____

ONLINE RESOURCE

Ten tips on how to get more interviews

People who don't get interviews don't get jobs and, worse still in many ways, they feel they've failed. If not getting interviews is your problem, you can access a free download with ten useful tips. Go to the following website:

www.TYCoachbooks.com/Interviews

4 WHAT TO DO BEFORE AN INTERVIEW

OUTCOMES FROM THIS CHAPTER

- Know what you need to do before you go for an interview.
- Understand how to research employers so you know more about what to expect.
- Think about the important messages you need to get across (the messages that will enhance your chances of getting the job).
- Know what questions you need to ask.

BEING INVITED TO AN INTERVIEW

Sometimes interviews are fixed up over the phone. Sometimes a letter or an email arrives giving you a time and date on which to attend and asking you to reply to confirm that the arrangement is suitable. Sometimes the letter or email will ask you to ring in to make an appointment.

Handling phone calls to employers

When you are asked to call in to fix up an interview, do just that. Don't tarnish your image by protracting the conversation with unnecessary digressions. Just because you've got the ear of an employer doesn't give you licence to start asking a thousand and one questions. Don't, whatever you do, start asking questions like 'Can you tell me more about the salary so I can decide whether I want to come or not?' There is a time and a place for questions and this isn't it. Worse still, you can start to undo the good work you've done so far by coming across as one of those people who don't know when to get off the phone.

Your first voice contact with an employer is therefore important and, generally speaking, the less you say the better. Be friendly and engaging by all means, but remember that the person on the other end of the line is probably sitting in the middle of a busy office dealing with all sorts of conflicting issues, so don't take up any more of their time than necessary.

Creating a good first impression

It's a good idea, too, to say thank you for the invitation to attend the interview. Observing common courtesy goes a long way when it comes to creating a good first impression. Remember the lesson in Chapter 1. A bad first impression, like a good one, has a tendency to stick.

COACHING SESSION 26

The ten jobs you need to do

Make a list of what you consider to be the ten most important jobs to do before you go to an interview. Record them here.

1 _____

2 _____

3 _____

4 _____

5 _____

6 _____

7 _____

8 _____

9 _____

10 _____

CONFIRMING INTERVIEWS

Even though you have fixed up the time and date for an interview over the phone, it is still a good idea to confirm in writing what has been arranged. There are two reasons for this:

1. It prevents misunderstandings arising. The time and date of the interview are recorded in black and white and don't rely on anyone's memory of what was agreed verbally in a phone conversation.

2. It looks professional and businesslike, and provides a further extension of the good first impression you've worked so hard to create.

DECIDING WHAT TO WEAR

Still on the subject of making a good first impression, the next item on the agenda is deciding what clothes to wear when you go for an interview. What standards of dress do interviewers expect and how do your ideas on what to wear fit in with theirs?

COACHING SESSION 27

The art of dressing

Imagine you've applied for the position of Head of Finance with a well-known company. You've now been invited to attend a preliminary interview with the consultant who has been retained to advise on the appointment.

List here what you consider to be important when it comes to choosing what clothes to wear.

_____

_____

_____

_____

_____

Dress codes

The days have long gone when it was the unwritten rule that you wore your Sunday best when you went for an interview. Today, the world of work is more relaxed when it comes to dress codes but this, in a way, makes the job of choosing clothes for interviews even more difficult. If you dress too casually, could it make the interviewer think you haven't bothered to make an effort? On the other hand, if you over-dress could you come across as formal and starchy?

Here is a list of tips for getting it right:

- **Choose clothes consistent with the job for which you are applying.**

In coaching session 27 the interview was for a senior management position in finance where standard business attire (dark suit etc.) would be expected and, if not worn, could attract negative attention. On the other hand, if you're applying for a job that calls for you to be hands-on in a factory some of the time, then to be dressed in the same way could suggest to the interviewer that you're not the sort to get your sleeves rolled up, so here a more casual style of dress would be more appropriate.

- **Make sure that you choose clothes that are smart.**

Even the dark suit won't look good if it's creased. If 'smart casual' is more suitable, it's still best to err on the side of smart rather than casual. And casual doesn't mean sloppy or shabby.

- **Make sure that your clothes are clean.**

Yesterday's shirt or blouse won't do anything for you on the first impressions front. This rule also applies to shoes – interviewers still look at candidates' shoes to see whether they have been polished.

- **Show your individuality.**

As discussed in Chapter 1, try to wear something which is a little different and which says something about you – without going over the top. Where candidates are seen in succession (as in the case of preliminary interviews), interviewers often bring people back to mind by reference to something they wore. These points of recollection are important. Otherwise your face could start to blur in with all the rest.

- **Make sure that your clothes – and you – smell fresh.**

Don't store your clothes near where they could pick up nasty smells. A waft of stale cigarettes is a definite turn-off, especially if the interviewer is a non-smoker. The same goes for the smell of last night's fry-up.

Feeling overdressed

What you would do if you arrived for an interview in a smart suit, only to find that your interviewer was wearing a casual shirt, jeans and trainers? This, you will remember, was one of the questions in the coaching session at the start of the book.

Feeling overdressed is one thing, but imagine how you would feel if the positions were reversed. So don't, whatever you do, try to rectify the situation by turning up for your next interview in clothes you normally wear on Saturday afternoons. Not allowing interviewers who dress down to distract you from the job you're there to do is all part of handling the diversity of interview scenarios.

QQ COACHING SESSION 28

Getting expert advice on dress

Usually, no one will give you advice on your clothes and appearance unless you ask and, sadly for most candidates whose appearance is letting them down, they're the last to find out – if they ever do. This is why it is good to seek out someone who can give you expert advice.

Do you know anyone who:

- interviews candidates for jobs on a regular basis?
- would be frank enough to give you an honest opinion on where you might benefit from spending a little money on your wardrobe?

List them here.

_____

_____

_____

_____

_____

_____

Grooming

Since you want to project an image of someone who will be an acceptable presence in the workplace, you will need to pay attention to your personal grooming as part of your preparation for going to an interview. Greasy or unkempt hair won't give a good first impression, nor will any odours, so invest in a good-quality deodorant (one that is effective without being strong smelling). However, avoid overpowering perfumes and aftershaves, which many people find off-putting.

PLANNING YOUR INTERVIEW DAY

One of the most unpredictable things about interviews is their length. At one extreme you could be in and out in 15 to 20 minutes, and at the other an interview could go on for two or three hours. While shortlist interviews will tend to be longer than preliminaries and interviews for senior positions will tend to be longer than interviews for jobs lower down the ladder, there are still no certainties.

However, what this means in practice is that you should never make any arrangement which is going to put pressure on you during an interview – for example having to collect children or be back at work for a certain time. You should also bear in mind that interviews frequently run late and, while it may not be your fault, you won't do much for your chances if you have to excuse yourself halfway through or, if you're sweating to get off, you're not concentrating on what the interviewer is saying.

Journey planning

Arriving late for an interview is the classic bad start. It creates a first impression that is unfortunate, to say the least. Employers are not well disposed towards latecomers and they probably have their share already, in the shape of employees at various stages of their disciplinary procedures.

COACHING SESSION 29

Being on time

Before you go to the interview, what can you do to help yourself avoid the embarrassment of turning up late?

Write your answer here.

_____

_____

_____

_____

_____

_____

Dummy runs

If the interview is reasonably local to where you live and you intend to travel by car, you can do a dummy run to see:

- how long the journey takes
- where on the journey there is the potential for traffic hold-ups.

> **! COACH'S TIP**
>
> **Allow for heavy traffic**
>
> If you do your dummy run at an off-peak time and if your interview is taking place during normal office hours, then make allowances for daytime traffic. Make allowances, too, for hold-ups on motorways.

Car parking

One of the main reasons why people arrive late for interviews is because they can't find anywhere to park. As part of your preparations for an interview, therefore, always investigate the availability of parking and, at the same time, have a contingency plan for the situation where you arrive and find all parking spaces taken. Contingency plans could include investigating the availability of on-street parking within reasonable walking distance.

Alternatives to travelling by car

Because of the unpredictability of modern traffic conditions and parking – especially in city centres – it may pay to consider:

- travelling by public transport, if it is available
- taking a taxi
- getting someone to give you a lift.

CVs, COVER LETTERS AND APPLICATION FORMS

When you go for an interview, it is customary to find the interviewer seated behind a desk with your CV and cover letter in front of him or her. If at any point you have been asked to complete an application form, then it is also customary to find that this is also on the interviewer's desk.

Unless the interviewer has previous knowledge of you – for example, if you've worked for the same organization before – your CV, cover letter and application form will be the starting point for the dialogue that is about to open up. The interviewer will be assessing your suitability for the job in question and the information in your CV, cover letter and application form will determine:

- the direction of the interview
- the topics that come up for discussion
- the questions that are asked.

Interviewers frequently cast their eyes over candidates' cover letters, CVs and application forms just before the interview starts. Therefore the information they've just read is freshest in their minds and, for this reason, it will be the natural lead-in point to the interview.

! COACH'S TIP

Revisit your cover letter, CV and application form

Instead of rehearsing answers to the kind of tough questions that form the basis of much of the literature on interviews, you will make far better use of your time by rereading your cover letter, CV and application form, for two reasons:

1　Their content will often give you clues to the direction the interview will go in.

2　By reminding yourself what you've said in these documents, you will be less likely to fall into the trap of contradicting yourself.

FINDING OUT MORE ABOUT EMPLOYERS

One of the questions you are frequently asked at interviews is 'What do you know about us?' Doing some research before you go to an interview is therefore recommended, for the following reasons:

- You can plan how you would answer this question if it were put to you.
- You can add to your store of knowledge of how the company would rate as a prospective employer.

COACHING SESSION 30

Doing your research

How would you go about researching prospective employers?

List the ways you can think of here.

1 _____

_____

_____

2 _____

_____

_____

3 _____

_____

_____

4 _____

_____

_____

5 _____

_____

_____

The Internet

The Internet is an obvious source of information on employers – and not only from their websites. By doing a search, you may also pick up other interesting snippets such as news articles or comments on their products and services. In the case of a public company, you will probably find a set of their Annual Report & Accounts included in their website, which will give you interesting insights into how the business is performing. Note, too, that employees who want to air complaints about their company often use social media, but don't be put off by what you read.

Networking

While you may not want to divulge the reason for your interest, don't overlook your circle of friends and business contacts as providers of information. It is from sources such as these that you may pick up all sorts of interesting titbits – not just what the employer's website would have you believe. If you can tap into someone who works for the employer or who has worked for them previously, then you will be able to get information from the horse's mouth. But, again, beware of individuals who want to air a grievance.

Recruitment consultants

If you've sourced the interview by being registered with a firm of recruitment consultants (an employment agency), they should be able to give you some background both on the employer and the job for which you are applying. Take care, though, because most recruitment consultants operate on a 'no placement, no fee' basis, meaning that it's very much in their interest to see that you get the job. Expect, therefore, to be painted rosy pictures.

The ad for the job

When you apply for a job that has been advertised in the press or on a website, keep a copy of what you saw and refer to it again before you go to the interview. While most ads don't give much detail, they often contain some information about the employer that is relevant to the job and for this reason they are worth revisiting.

FINDING OUT MORE ABOUT INTERVIEWERS

In the previous chapter you saw how difficult it is to predict what is going to happen at an interview. What would help you, of course, would be, in advance of going to an interview, knowing more about:

- the interviewer's competence at handling interviews
- the kind of questions you are likely to be asked.

COACHING SESSION 31

Types of interviewer

What differences would you expect to see between an interview conducted by a professional such as an HR manager and an interview conducted by a line manager?

List them here.

_____

_____

_____

_____

_____

_____

_____

_____

Professionals vs. line managers

If you are told that your interview will be with a professional such as an HR manager or a consultant, it is reasonable to expect the interview to follow a standard path. In most cases, a professional will have only a limited appreciation of the work you do, so the questions asked will tend to be general rather than ones that probe into the detail of your job knowledge. Interviews with professionals are usually well organized and run to time.

An interview with a line manager won't be so easy to predict. The line manager will be someone who heads up the team in the part of the organization where the vacant position is based. You will be asked questions about what you know and less emphasis will be placed on your character and motivation. These managers are often unused to carrying out interviews and so they may be less disciplined in their approach than a professional.

These observations on what to expect at interviews are generalizations and there are always exceptions to the rule (as Olivia's experience with Al demonstrated). Furthermore, interviews that run late are not always the interviewer's fault. Sometimes the cause is an earlier candidate who didn't arrive on time.

COACHING SESSION 32

Deciding the important messages you need to get across

When planning your strategy for an interview, you need to decide on what are the important messages you want to get across in the time allocated to you.

Go back to the last job application you made and look at what you felt you had to offer that made you an ideal candidate for the job.

1. Make a list here of all the points.

1 _____

2 _____

3 _____

4 _____

5 _____

6 _____

7 _____

8 _____

Now look at your list and count the number of points. Are there more than six? If there are, go through the list and strike out any that are not relevant to the job for which you have applied.

2. Now list the top six in rank order, with the most important at number one and so on.

1 _____

2 _____

3 _____

4 _____

5 _____

6 _____

You now have six or fewer key matches between what you have to offer and what the employer sought to see in candidates for the job. These are your important messages and the point to restricting them to six or fewer is to make it feasible to get them across within the space of a 45-minute interview.

INTERVIEWERS' QUESTIONS

Some interviewers are disposed towards asking quirky questions of the kind that no one could ever be expected to predict. Apart from following the standard guidance of being prepared for anything when you go for an interview, is there any way of knowing what questions an interviewer is fond of asking so you're not caught out by the offbeat or the unusual and you can prepare an answer?

Do you know anybody who has been to an interview with the interviewer before? If so, it's worth putting out a few feelers to find out what questions were asked.

Again, if you've been put forward for the job by a firm of recruitment consultants, you can tap into their knowledge. Their information about interviewers' idiosyncrasies will be based in most cases on feedback from candidates who have been for interviews before. This time, the consultants' wish to see you get the job works in your favour. Providing you ask them, they will give you any help they can to help you deal with unusual or tricky questions, even down to suggesting the best way to answer them.

The next chapter (Chapter 5) deals with interview questions in more detail.

WHERE YOUR COVER LETTER AND CV COME IN

If you've done a good job with the design of your cover letter and CV, these important messages will have already been given prominence. Since cover letters and CVs will dictate the agendas for interviews, you can now let these documents do the work for you. Leave it to interviewers to cast their eyes over your cover letter and CV and pick out the aspects that interest them – which of your messages they want to talk about.

In this way, your cover letter and CV act as menus from which the interviewer can pick and choose items. Every item on the menu is, of course, one that is favourable to you. The only part you have to play in the process is therefore to keep your eye on how the interview is unfolding. If the content of your cover letter and CV are leading the interviewer, all should go well, but if the interviewer seems to be straying from it, this may call for input from you. There is more on making sure that the important messages have been delivered elsewhere in this book.

DECIDING WHAT QUESTIONS TO ASK

As you have seen, interviews are a two-way process. Employers need to find out more about you and you need to find out more about them – much more than you already know.

COACHING SESSION 33

What you need to know

The point of this exercise is to prepare a list of questions ready for when you are next called to an interview. Your list of questions is one of the documents you will be taking to the interview with you.

What would you need to know about a job before you took it? Make a list of what you feel would be important questions to ask.

1 _____

_____

2 _____

_____

3 _____

_____

4 _____

_____

5 _____

_____

6 _____

_____

COACH'S TIP

Your list of questions

When you print off your list of questions before going to an interview, leave spaces between each question so you can write in the answers. Also see the list as one you will add to as you gain more interview experience.

COACHING SESSION 34

Two important questions

Two important questions to ask are:

- 'What do you see as the important qualities for this job?'
- 'What happened to the last person?'

1. Why is it important to ask these questions?

_____

_____

_____

_____

_____

_____

_____

_____

_____

_____

2. What will you learn from the answers and how will the information be helpful to you?

_____

_____

_____

_____

_____

_____

_____

_____

_____

_____

_____

Getting the employer's take on what they see as the important attributes for the job will help you plan for the next stage. You will know what you need to focus on if you have the good fortune to be asked back for another interview.

Knowing what happened to the last incumbent may give you some interesting insights into the inner workings of the organization. If the last person retired or got a better job somewhere else, then fine, but if there was a dismissal (or one is pending), it will be interesting to hear what the interviewer has to say about it. In this case, the more you're told the better because, if someone has had the sack, the next person to do the job might have to start by clearing up the mess left behind. This could be you, of course.

BE READY TO SAY YES

The purpose of getting answers to your questions is so that you have enough information to be able to decide whether to accept the job or not if it is offered to you. If you don't have enough information to make this decision, you will be faced with a problem (one that will be discussed later in the book).

You also need to bear in mind that, in today's strange and unpredictable world, interviews can sometimes end with you being offered the job there and then. You are put on the spot by being asked whether you will accept the offer. You can always buy time by asking for a few days to think it over, but a lot can happen in a few days and clinching the deal while it's there and available has a lot to be said for it.

→ NEXT STEPS

This chapter has been about jobs you need to do before you go to an interview. These are:

- confirming that you will be attending and doing nothing to undermine the favourable first impression you have formed

- planning for the practicalities of the interview day itself, including what to wear

- finding out more about the employer and the person who will be interviewing you

- deciding what there is about you that will give you the best chance of getting the job (the messages you need to get across)

- deciding what you need to know about the job so you will be able to determine whether it's one you would accept if it were offered to you.

Being ready for what could happen to you on the day is important. Interviews are unpredictable enough, so anything you can do to be prepared for what could be coming your way will work in your favour.

The next chapter deals with the subject of interview questions:

- What you will be asked

- What's behind the questions

- The right way to answer them.

👍 TAKEAWAYS

Has reading this chapter taught you anything new about how to respond to employers who invite you to an interview – anything that hasn't occurred to you before? Is it information that you will find useful?

_____

_____

_____

_____

_____

_____

_____

_____

_____

Did you find the section on what to wear for an interview helpful? Was there anything you hadn't considered before? Will you dress differently next time you go for an interview? If so, in what way?

_____

_____

_____

_____

_____

_____

_____

_____

_____

Similarly, was the advice about journey planning helpful? How will you change your travel plans next time you go for an interview?

_____

_____

_____

_____

_____

_____

_____

_____

_____

_____

Have you had the experience of running late on your journey to an interview? What did you do at the time and, in hindsight, was it the right action to take? Given the same situation again, what would you do differently?

_____

_____

_____

_____

_____

_____

_____

_____

_____

_____

_____

Few candidates think to revisit their cover letters, CVs and application forms before they go to interviews. Did you find the advice to do this useful? Is it something that you will make a point of doing in the future?

_____

_____

_____

_____

_____

_____

_____

_____

_____

_____

As a result of reading this chapter, have you learned anything new about researching employers? Was there anything you hadn't considered previously?

_____

_____

_____

_____

_____

_____

_____

_____

_____

_____

_____

_____

Has reading the chapter given you any ideas on how you can be better prepared for the questions interviewers ask? List your ideas here.

_____

_____

_____

_____

_____

_____

Has the section on deciding what questions you need to ask given you any food for thought? Are there any questions you neglected to ask when you last went for an interview? Write them down here to act as a reminder for next time.

_____

_____

_____

_____

_____

_____

_____

ONLINE RESOURCE

Go to your interviews

After doing all the hard work of getting an interview, there are always people who either don't show up or who phone in with some lame excuse. Find out more about what's behind this seemingly strange behaviour in a free download, which you can access by going to the website below.

www.TYCoachbooks.com/Interviews

INTERVIEW QUESTIONS

OUTCOMES FROM THIS CHAPTER

- Learn how to handle the questions that interviewers ask.
- Understand what's behind the questions.
- Know how to deal with the questions that interviewers don't ask.

THOSE FREQUENTLY ASKED QUESTIONS

Every interview is different. Every interviewer is different. This is why it is impossible to predict all the questions you are going to be asked at an interview. However, some questions do come up so frequently that it is worth spending a few minutes considering them and, more importantly, considering how you would answer them if they were put to you.

COACHING SESSION 35

Likely questions

Have a go at guessing some of the questions you're most likely to be asked when you next go for an interview. List ten of them here:

1 _____

_____

_____

2 _____

_____

_____

3

_____

_____

4

_____

_____

5

_____

_____

6

_____

_____

7

_____

_____

8

_____

_____

9

_____

_____

10

_____

_____

'What do you know about us?'

At some point during the interview, the interviewer will want to tell you about the organization and the job for which you're applying. Finding out how much you know already will tell him or her where to start. They also ask this question because they want to know how much pre-interview research you've done because it is a useful measure of your interest in the job.

COACHING SESSION 36

'What do you know about the organization?'

Use the space below to set down a few bullet points on how you would go about answering this question.

_____

_____

_____

_____

_____

_____

The best way to deal with the question is to answer as follows:

- To show what research you've done, tell the interviewer where the information you're quoting comes from (for example, the organization's website or its latest set of published accounts).

- Stick to the good points.

- Give your answer in three or four sentences.

- Say that the organization sounds like one you would like to work for.

'Why are you applying for this job?'

Interviewers will ask you why you're applying for the job for two main reasons:

1. To get some insight into your motivation and what drives you

This is important when they are trying to form a view on how you would respond to certain job situations. For example, someone applying for a job in commission-only sales needs to be motivated by money. On the other hand, someone with a big money motivation wouldn't be suitable for a position where looking after others or quality of finished work is the prime objective.

2. To form a view on whether the job matches up with what you're looking for

This is where the interviewer and you share the same concerns. If the job is a mismatch and doesn't line up with your ambitions, the sooner everyone finds out the better.

COACHING SESSION 37

'Why do you want this job?'

Use the space below to set down a few bullet points on how you would go about answering this question.

_____

_____

_____

_____

_____

_____

The best way to deal with the question is to answer as follows:

- Keep the reply brief.

- Tell the interviewer how you see the job fitting in with what you've said about your aims and ambitions in your cover letter and CV.

COACH'S TIP

What *not* to say

1. Whatever you do, don't reply to the question 'Why are you applying for this job?' with a long list of grumbles about your present job. However much the grumbling is justified, interviewers understandably don't warm to people who come across as complainers.

2. Don't say you've applied because you're out of work or at risk of redundancy, either. It implies you're desperate and anything will do – which is not what interviewers want to hear.

'Why do you want to leave your current job?'

The reasons are more or less the same as the reasons for asking you why you're applying for the job. Your answer will

- give clues to your motivation

- help to expose any mismatches.

For example, if your reason for wanting to leave your current job is because you are having to spend long periods of time away from home and if the job you're applying for has a similar requirement, there is no point in proceeding further. In a perfect world, a mismatch such as this would have been picked up earlier. Your CV would have flagged up your reason for wanting to make a move and whoever put the interview list together would have seen it. The world of interviews is, however, far from perfect!

COACHING SESSION 38

'Why leave your current job?'

What would you say in response to this question? Record your answers here.

_____

_____

_____

_____

_____

The best way to deal with the question is to answer as follows:

- Be concise and consistent with what you have said about yourself in your CV and cover letter.

- Be positive about your current job and give positive reasons for wanting to leave it.

It's important to avoid grumbling about your present job. Here are a few examples of the right and wrong ways of saying the same thing.

The wrong way	The right way
'They expect me to work for peanuts.'	'I think my skills might be better rewarded.'
'I'm in a dead-end job with a dead-end outfit.'	'I'm looking to join a more progressive organization where, if I work hard, I will have better prospects.'
'They don't do anything about training. They're not interested in people, only in themselves.'	'I want a job where I will be able to advance my career through better training opportunities.'
'They've never heard of please and thank you.'	'I would like to work for a more professionally managed organization.'

The trick in each case is to turn the negative into the positive and to focus attention on where you want to go next, rather than on the problems of where you are now.

'Why did you leave your last job?'

If you are out of work for any reason, such as redundancy, the question 'Why do you want to leave?' will be replaced by 'Why did you leave?' – referring of course to your last job.

In today's climate, redundancy is the main reason people find themselves out of work. They lost their job because the branch where they worked closed down or the business which employed them for ten years was hit by a global decline in the demand for its products, or something else happened which was no fault of theirs.

However, be warned that interviewers often want to go behind the reasons for redundancy. This is because selection for redundancy is sometimes based on job performance or attendance record and the interviewer will be keen to establish that you don't fall into one of these categories. Some candidates apply the term 'redundancy' to any loss of job situation, so, for example, you find people who have been dismissed for misconduct saying that they have been made redundant.

If you have given redundancy as the reason why you lost your last job, be ready to answer these more detailed questions:

- What brought the redundancy about (e.g. closure of the part of the business where you were based)?
- How many others were made redundant?
- Why were you selected (what criteria were used)?

'Where do you see yourself in five years' time?'

The classic answer to this question is 'Sitting in your seat', which is fine if the interviewer happens to be the person who would be your boss if you got the job. It wouldn't make sense if the interviewer is the employer's HR manager and you're not from an HR background. One candidate answered the question by saying with a smile, 'You tell me.' Perhaps your ideas are better! Again, keep the answer concise.

COACHING SESSION 39

'Where do you see yourself five years from now?'

If it were put to you, how would you answer this question? What, in your view, would be a good and bad answer to the question? In both cases, explain your reasons why.

1. A good answer:

_____

_____

_____

_____

2. A bad answer:

_____

_____

_____

_____

_____

'What are your strengths and weaknesses?'

The aim in asking you this question is partly to put a bit of pressure on you and partly to see how good you are at thinking on your feet. What you say about yourself in reply needs to be:

- consistent with anything you've said about yourself elsewhere (CV, cover letter, application form, social networking sites, etc.)

- relevant to the job for which you're applying

- concise.

Asking you to say what your strengths are gives you a perfect opportunity, of course, to lay out or reiterate your important messages. Talking about your weaknesses is harder, for the simple reason that your weaknesses are not what you want the discussion to focus on. Clearly, what you won't be doing therefore is attracting attention to any aspect of your character that would cause the interviewer to have doubts about your suitability for the job. An example of a good answer about weaknesses was when one candidate came up with 'chocolate'. See if you can better it.

COACHING SESSION 40

Your strengths and weaknesses

How would you answer the question about these if it were put to you? Can you think of what you should and shouldn't say?

1. Strengths

A good answer:

_____

_____

_____

_____

A bad answer:

_____

_____

_____

_____

2. Weaknesses

A good answer:

_____

_____

_____

_____

A bad answer:

_____

_____

_____

_____

'Tell me a bit about yourself.'

If you're not expecting it, this is the kind of opener to an interview that could throw you into a spin. Why are interviewers fond of throwing the floor over to you in this way? The answer is that it gets you talking and gives the interviewer a chance to sit back and listen.

Be aware, though, that being asked to tell an interviewer a bit more about yourself should never be taken as an invitation to launch into a 20-minute oral version of your CV. If you do, you will find not only that you waste precious interview time but also that the interviewer switches off because what you are saying isn't relevant to the line of enquiry they wish to pursue. Try therefore to respond without getting into a lot of detail. Stick to the main messages you want to get across. Most importantly, keep it brief.

BACKGROUND QUESTIONS

These are often questions about the practicalities of how you would do the job, as well as seemingly more personal questions. Employers sometimes simply want to find out more about you to get a feel for your character, but in most cases the questions will have greater relevance.

Your domestic circumstances

Questions about those you share your life with and who is dependent on you (e.g. are you responsible for any children?) often figure at interviews. For example, if you are applying for a job that will involve spending long periods of time overseas and you are only recently married, employers will want to know more about whether you and your partner have thought this through properly. Expect therefore more vigorous questions where there is a seeming conflict between your domestic circumstances and the requirements of the job. Most importantly, have your answers ready and make sure that they are convincing.

Getting to work

Of concern to employers are people who take on long or difficult journeys to work (because they need the job), but then find that the daily routine becomes too much for them. The result is that they find another job nearer their home and then leave. The employer is then put into the position of having to go back to square one and find someone else suitable to fill the post. Any investment in training has been a waste of money.

COACHING SESSION 41

Your journey to work

In the following scenario, the candidate is being interviewed for a job where the daily journey to work would involve spending over an hour on the road.

Interviewer: You live a long way away. What about travelling to work every day? How long would it take you?

Answer A: I don't mind driving.

Answer B: Just over an hour. I timed the journey on the way here today. Door to door, my current journey to work takes about 50 minutes so it's not very different.

1. What, in your opinion, is wrong with Answer A?

2. Why is Answer B better?

Answer B shows not only that the candidate has given some thought to daily travel but also deals with the interviewer's concern. Answer A does neither.

Your legal right to work in the country

A question about your right to take up employment will feature in the interview if you originate from another country. Taking relevant documents to the interview, such as work permits, will help clear up any concerns on this score straight away. Note that the interviewer will probably want to take photocopies of any documents you produce.

Your driving licence

Where the job involves travel and/or the use of a company vehicle, questions about your driving licence will probably be part of standard procedure. Interviewers may ask to see your driving licence, so it is a good idea to take it with you.

> ## ! COACH'S TIP
>
> ### Warning!
> Don't try to explain away any road traffic offences ('It was a bit of bad luck – the traffic cop was parked just round the corner'). Employers are not impressed by people who make excuses.

Your family background

Candidates who find themselves being asked what their mothers and fathers do (or did) for a living are often confused about the reason why. Some candidates go so far as to ask the interviewer to explain the relevance of the question.

Don't think that, by asking you about your family background, interviewers are prying into an area of your life that you view as private. For example, a common mistake candidates make is to see themselves at a disadvantage if they don't come from the same background as the interviewer, if this seems to be a more middle-class or wealthy one, whereas the reverse is probably true. Where you came from, if you had to struggle to get qualifications and rise thorough the ranks from a deprived background, says a lot about you and your motivation. Be proud of your origins. Let the world see that you are a fighter and an achiever.

COACHING SESSION 42

The relevance of family background

Not all interviewers ask about a candidate's family background but, for those who do, suggest a reason why parental occupations might have a bearing on assessing someone's suitability for a job.

_____

_____

_____

_____

_____

_____

_____

_____

_____

_____

COACH'S TIP

Your background

Questions about family background are more likely to be put to you if you are a younger candidate without much of a work track record to go on. The information you give will help the interviewer form a view of your motivation.

Your education

Again, the younger you are (and especially if you are under 25), the more likely you are to be asked questions about your education. This is simply because it forms the bigger part of your life so far. Expect questions about why you chose to pursue certain courses of study.

COACHING SESSION 43

Talking about a course of study

In this scenario, a candidate has been asked why she decided to study for a degree in psychology. Here are two possible replies she could give:

Reply A: 'It was my best subject at school. I thought that if I did psychology it would give me the best chance of coming out of university with a first-class honours degree.'

Reply B: 'I thought psychology would give me a good foundation for a career in human resources management. That was the main reason I chose it.'

Suggest in your own words why reply B is better than reply A.

_____

_____

_____

_____

_____

_____

Your leisure time

Some interviewers will ask you about what you get up to when you are not at work and, on the face of it, such questions seem innocent enough. However, be aware that in a world where employers increasingly expect a high level of personal commitment, interests and hobbies that could get in the way of work are not welcome. Here are a few 'don'ts' on how to answer questions about what you do in your leisure time:

- **Don't** talk at length about what you do in your spare time because, apart from taking up interview time, it suggests that you might put your interests before the job if conflict arose.

- **Don't** lay down conditions to employers. For example:

  - Interviewer: 'We do stocktakes at the end of every quarter, when employees are expected to work weekends. Could this give you a problem?'

  - Candidate: 'Only in the football season, when I play for a team on Saturday afternoons.'

- **Don't** list dangerous pastimes that may result in injuries and you having to take time off work.

- **Don't** give long lists of outside activities, or you will have the interviewer wondering how you manage to fit in going to work.

COACHING SESSION 44

What do you do in your leisure time?

Can you suggest a reason why you need to be extra careful about talking at length about leisure-time activities when you have been out of work for a period of time?

_____

_____

_____

_____

_____

YOUR EMPLOYMENT HISTORY

Questions about your employment history will probably take up most of the interview, because this is what is most relevant to the job you are applying for. You are likely to be asked questions about the jobs you have done, the experience you have gained, and why, when it came to it, you chose to move on.

As suggested earlier in the chapter, have answers ready for the following questions:

- 'Why did you leave [your previous jobs]?'

- 'Why do you want to leave [your present job]?'

Avoid negative answers to these questions, such as 'My boss is an idiot'. Your boss may well be an idiot, but to someone who doesn't know you it could be an indicator that you are difficult to manage.

Get ready to flesh out the information you give when the reason was or is redundancy.

Reasons for leaving jobs

Apart from getting a better understanding of the range of your experience, employers will be trying to pick up clues – from your reasons for leaving jobs – about:

- what makes you tick
- how much you will put up with
- whether you have failed in any of the jobs (an indicator that you could fail again).

COACHING SESSION 45

Looking at a track record

In this scenario, the interviewer is interviewing a well-qualified candidate but has noticed on his application form that:

- he doesn't spend long in jobs
- his reason for leaving is always 'better money'.

Now put yourself in the interviewer's place and ask yourself what this track record is suggesting about the candidate.

Write your answer here.

_____

_____

_____

_____

_____

_____

Salary reasons for leaving jobs are understandable. Everyone aspires to be better paid. However, a candidate who is constantly on the move for more money conveys the image of someone perpetually shopping around and therefore not necessarily the best person to have on the team. If an interviewer asks you why you left a particular job, it's fine to say that they offered you more money, but was this because you applied to them or did they approach you? If it was the latter, it would be best to say so. This then dispels the impression that you spend your spare time going round searching for better-paid jobs.

A question mark could also be put over a candidate who gives 'improved prospects' as the reason for moving jobs, when the new job doesn't seem all that different from the old one – the move doesn't make sense. If, as so many people do, you saw moving sideways as the eventual means to moving upwards, this would be worth explaining to the interviewer so that you can dispel the impression that you are a drifter with no defined aims or ambitions.

> **! COACH'S TIP**
>
> ### Us and them
>
> When you are talking about previous employers, use 'we' and 'us' rather than 'they' and 'them'. It then sounds as if you were part of the team rather than a bystander who contributed nothing.

QUESTIONS INTERVIEWERS DON'T ASK

Interviewers don't always ask the questions they need to ask and thus they fail to get the full picture of what a candidate knows or can do. If this happens to you, you will need to take action to ensure that you get your vital messages across. Input from you is, as you have learned already, all part of the principle of **keeping control.**

In the scenario that follows, a candidate is being interviewed for a job where knowledge of a certain type of software (X) is a requirement.

Interviewer: 'I want to talk about your experience with software. You have been with Snodgrass & Snippet for the past two years; what kind of software do you use?'

Candidate: 'Mainly Y.'

Interviewer: 'What about X?'

Candidate: 'There has been talk about buying a package but no decisions have been taken yet.'

....

Interviewer: 'What about your previous job with Wanless & Wistance? What software did you use there?'

Candidate: X. 'I used it every day for six-and-a-half years.'

The significance of the dotted line in the script is that some interviewers would end their line of questioning at that point. If they did, they would form the incorrect view that the candidate has no experience of using X.

The candidate therefore needs to see:

- what is behind the line of questioning
- the interviewer's omission
- that, to prevent an incorrect view being formed, some input from him is required.

The input in this case would consist of the candidate expanding his answer to the interviewer's original question about his experience in his current job.

! COACH'S TIP

Tell the whole story

Interviewers who only get half the story and then move on do so either because they are not used to interviewing or because they don't give interviews enough time and have to rush things. Being on your toes in case some vital part of your experience is overlooked is all part of being successful at interviews in a world of inconsistent standards.

Questions interviewers are unable to ask

In some countries, a potential employer is not allowed by law to ask certain questions. These are usually questions that have no bearing on your ability to do the job, such as those that relate to your marital status. This is deemed to be especially discriminatory towards women who are married, as employers may choose not to employ them because of the outdated notion of women as primary caregivers to children.

ΩΩ COACHING SESSION 46

Addressing a perceived conflict

Imagine that you are a female applicant for a job where you will be required to travel anywhere in the world at the drop of a hat and that on some of these trips you could be away from home for weeks at a time. Imagine, too, that you are also the mother of two preschool-age children. What, on the face of it, looks like a conflict in fact isn't: your partner is happy to act in the role of househusband and it fits in nicely with the work he does as an illustrator of children's books.

You have now been for an interview where the interviewer (male, and one of the directors of the business where the job is based) was upbeat and went so far as to say that you stood a good chance of being offered the job. The interview itself was quite short and you found it pleasing that no questions were asked about your domestic situation. However, you have now received a letter turning you down for the job.

What are your thoughts? Record them here.

_____

_____

_____

_____

_____

_____

_____

_____

_____

_____

_____

Thinking that you didn't get the job because of your domestic situation may be incorrect, but it stands a fair chance that the potential conflict between being the mother of two small children and travelling all over the world might have played some part in the decision. If so, what you have probably witnessed here is that the interviewer saw the potential conflict but felt unable to probe any further into how you saw it being resolved. He probably sensed that he was straying into dangerous territory (gender discrimination) and decided to play safe by steering clear of the subject altogether.

The problem for you, of course, is that the interview was your one chance of putting these concerns to bed. You didn't take control and, for this reason, it has to be said that some of the fault lies with you.

! COACH'S TIP

Face important issues head on

Spot the areas where interviewers may fight shy of asking important questions, either because they find the questions difficult or because they sense it could get them into trouble (with the candidate or with the law).

PRE-EMPTIVE STRIKES

The subject of pre-emptive strikes has come up already. Pre-emptive strikes are necessary only when information with a crucial bearing on you getting the job hasn't yet been imparted. For example, in the coaching session above, the role your partner took on in your domestic arrangements would not have been so crucial to the outcome of the interview if you had been applying for a normal 9–5 office job or one where the hours were part-time.

Be ready to make pre-emptive strikes where you:

- have any kind of domestic situation that is outside the norm
- have had several jobs in a short space of time
- have been dismissed
- keep being made redundant
- have a record of job moves that suggest you have been going sideways or downwards
- have anything else unusual about you that a prospective employer might view as an impediment.

→ NEXT STEPS

This chapter has been about dealing with the more obvious questions that come up at interviews and discovering:

- what's behind the questions

- the right and wrong way to go about answering them.

Although possible interview questions are so varied that there is no way you can anticipate all of them, it is useful to be aware that interview agendas are usually dictated by what interviewers have in front of them which, in most cases, will be:

- your cover letter and CV

- your application form, if you have been asked to fill one in.

By revisiting these documents you will therefore be able to pick up some useful clues on what line of questioning the interviewer is going to follow. Again, it illustrates the value of carrying out this exercise as part of your interview preparations.

You have also seen the importance of knowing how to deal with interviewers who don't ask the right questions. It may require some input from you, where you take control to ensure that you don't come away from the interview feeling that your best points didn't come across.

The next chapter explores the subject of preliminary interviews, where the challenge you face is being one of many candidates. It looks at how you can find some way of standing out from the crowd.

TAKEAWAYS

Did you find the information in this chapter on frequently asked questions helpful? When you next go to an interview, will you be making any changes to the way you answer these questions?

_____

_____

_____

_____

_____

_____

_____

_____

_____

In the light of what you have read in this chapter, do you think you could be letting yourself down with the reasons that you give to interviewers for leaving jobs? In what ways do you think you could improve your answers without distorting the truth?

_____

_____

_____

_____

_____

_____

_____

_____

_____

_____

What is your experience of being asked oddball questions at interviews? On closer inspection, were the questions really oddball or could you have anticipated them by being better prepared? Write down any thoughts.

_____

_____

_____

_____

_____

_____

_____

_____

_____

_____

Do you think you could improve some of the answers you have given in the past to questions about your background? How would you answer the same questions now?

_____

_____

_____

_____

_____

_____

_____

_____

_____

_____

_____

_____

Have you ever come away from an interview feeling that your best points didn't come across? If so, what will you be doing in future to ensure that this doesn't happen again?

_____

_____

_____

_____

_____

_____

_____

_____

_____

_____

_____

Did the section about questions interviewers don't ask give you any cause to reflect? Did you think of any areas where it might be advisable to consider a pre-emptive strike?

_____

_____

_____

_____

_____

_____

_____

_____

_____

_____

_____

_____

ONLINE RESOURCE

Skeletons in the cupboard

What if you've blotted your copybook a few times during the course of your career? How truthful should you be with interviewers? Access a free download to find out how to deal with the problem of what to say when you are asked questions about parts of your track record that you'd prefer to stay under wraps. Go to the following website:

www.TYCoachbooks.com/Interviews

6 | PRELIMINARY INTERVIEWS

✔ OUTCOMES FROM THIS CHAPTER

- Identify the challenges you face when you go for a preliminary interview.
- Know what to take with you.
- Understand what to do when it's your turn to ask questions.
- Know how to close the interview.

WHAT MAKES PRELIMINARY INTERVIEWS DIFFICULT?

👥 COACHING SESSION 47

The challenges of a preliminary interview

Based on your experience of going to preliminary interviews, can you think of four reasons why they are difficult to handle?

List them here.

1 _____

_____

2 _____

_____

3 _____

_____

4 _____

_____

How did you get on? Top marks if you got most or all of the following:

- **You are one of many.**

The purpose of a preliminary interview is to reduce the number of applicants for a job to a more manageable quantity. If you are invited to a preliminary interview, you are still therefore one of many. To get to the next stage, you will have to find some way of standing out from the crowd.

- **You have only a short time to make an impression.**

Preliminary interviews are normally kept short, so you will have only a limited amount of time to get your important messages across. Because it is usual for preliminary interviews to be done in succession, with one candidate being seen straight after another, interviewers will be keen not to let their interviews overrun.

- **You have to hold the interviewer's interest.**

Doing a succession of preliminary interviews can be tedious for interviewers and it is easy for them to lose concentration. Therefore, in addition to everything else you have to do, you also have to hold the interviewer's attention. Interviewers are not all blessed with perfect listening skills and some can and will switch off.

- **The interviewer may not know much about the work you do.**

Preliminary interviews are often done one-on-one, and it is not uncommon to find that the person sitting on the other side of the desk is someone from the human resources management team or a consultant brought in specially to advise. Such people are generalists and, unless you're applying for a job in human resources management, they won't have much knowledge of whatever it is that you do.

YOUR STRATEGY FOR PRELIMINARY INTERVIEWS

Some of these points have been touched on already, but they bear repeating:

- Keep your answers to questions short and concise. By going off on tangents, you could find that you start to lose the interviewer's attention as well as wasting precious interview time – time better spent talking about something that will enhance your chances of getting the job.

- On the subject of long rambles, don't take over interviews. Again, time will run out on you, so focus hard on getting those important messages across.

- Consistent with the need for brevity and concision, don't get into too much detail with your answers to questions. Anything technical or steeped in jargon will go right over the heads of interviewers if they are human resources specialists or outside consultants.

■ Remember that 'little bit of you', those glimpses of what makes you different that register with interviewers and help you stand out from the rest of the faces in the frame.

SUCCESS AT PRELIMINARY INTERVIEWS

To be successful at preliminary interviews, candidates have to pass two tests:

1. They must be capable of doing the job.

2. They must be seen as the kind of people who will 'fit in'.

Hidden criteria

Well-qualified candidates who are baffled about why they got no further than the preliminary interview stage for a job may find that the answer lies in the 'hidden criteria'. In many cases, hidden criteria exist because of employers' past experiences with people and they are often a feature of employment in small successful firms.

You can do nothing about hidden criteria. You won't even know they exist. For example, who will or won't fit in is largely a subjective judgement based, in many cases, on narrow perceptions of what will work in a particular environment.

An employer might think, but not say, 'When we get busy, everyone who works for us has to be prepared to put in the hours, which sometimes means working seven days a week. People with young families or people who like getting away at weekends don't therefore tend to last long.'

What candidates for this job won't be told, of course, is that anyone who wants any kind of life outside work doesn't stand a chance. However, they won't be told this because it doesn't project a very good image of the employer and, in some countries, it could be viewed as discriminatory. This is why such requirements are referred to as 'hidden criteria'.

Visual aids

In the case study in Chapter 3, Olivia compiled a portfolio of her best work. However, the mistake she made was with the presentation she rehearsed to go with her portfolio. It was too long, too detailed, and Al, the interviewer, had to cut her short. Furthermore, Al was a generalist, a human resources manager, so much of what Olivia was talking about went straight over his head.

People who work in visual professions such as design are used to the idea of taking along portfolios of their work to show prospective employers, but the rest of the population rarely think to do it. Pictures are worth a thousand words, so if you do have photographs of some of the work you have done or of products you have been associated with, take them along because they will avoid the need for long verbal descriptions. This is good for a number of reasons:

- Verbal descriptions, particularly when you're sitting in an interview, are quite hard. Your description may make sense to you and the interviewer may be nodding along, but the images forming in his or her head may, without you knowing it, be far removed from what you're trying to portray.

- There is a tendency to slip into jargon or technical terminology when you're talking about your job. This is where you lose interviewers who don't share your background.

- Long verbal descriptions take up valuable interview time.

🗪🗪 COACHING SESSION 48

What to take with you

Make a list here of what you would take with you to a preliminary interview.

1 _____

_____

2 _____

_____

3 _____

_____

4 _____

_____

5 _____

_____

Keep the items that you take into an interview to a minimum. There are two reasons for this:

- You don't want to be burdened down by items that are unnecessary.
- During the interview you could find yourself in the position of looking for something and not being able to find it.

COACHING SESSION 49

Your checklist

The following is a checklist of items to take with you when you go for a preliminary interview. Beside each item, write down why you think it is important.

Item	Why important
The letter or email inviting you to attend the interview or confirming the arrangement	
A notepad containing your list of questions and a pen	
Your pictures	
Copies of any certificates confirming qualifications relevant to the job	
A copy of your CV and cover letter	
Your driving licence (if you have one)	
Any necessary documents such as work permits and visas proving that it is legal for you to take up employment	
A mobile phone	
A broadsheet newspaper	

! COACH'S TIP

Turn off your phone!

Remember to switch your phone off as soon as you arrive at the employer's premises. Mobile phones going off during an interview rank highly among interviewers' pet hates and will also serve to put you off your stride.

ARRIVING ON TIME

As already mentioned, it's important to plan your journey to the interview so you don't have the embarrassment of arriving late (the classic bad start). Ideally, you should be aiming to arrive about ten minutes before the interview is due to start.

On the other hand, presenting yourself too early also has disadvantages:

- In a succession of interviews (especially those that are running late), you may have to wait with the candidate whose interview is before yours. Conversation could prove awkward and distract you from the important job of keeping your mind focused.

- You may have to wait a long time in an area with few creature comforts – even a cold draughty corridor with no seating.

- You may feel you're in the way and that you are being a nuisance.

If you find that you have allowed too much time for your journey to the interview and arrive more than 15 minutes early, consider either driving around the block a few times or sitting in the car and reading your newspaper. If you are very early, it might be best to find somewhere where you can relax over a cup of coffee.

What to do if you're late

This was one of the questions in coaching session 1 at the start of the book. What would you do if, on your journey to the interview, the traffic on the motorway came to a standstill and showed no signs of moving?

What you might feel in this situation is that you have lost your chance of the interview. However, everyone has been late for an appointment due to unforeseen circumstances and interviewers are no different from anyone else, so don't feel that all is lost. Get on the phone straight away and:

- apologize

- say you'll get there as quickly as you can

- say that, if this is a problem, you can come at another, more suitable time.

Long waits

When you go for a preliminary interview, there is always the possibility that you could be in for a long wait. The usual explanation is that a succession of candidates is being seen and one of them arrived late or an interview went on longer than expected. Sometimes you will be given the option of coming back later but, if not, you will just have to sit and wait. This is another situation where your newspaper will come in useful (better to be occupied than sit staring into space).

THE IMPORTANCE OF APPLICATION FORMS

In many organizations you will be invited to fill in a standard application form beforehand, but you may instead be presented with one only when you arrive for your interview. Never dismiss application forms or view them as pointless pieces of paperwork, which serve only to repeat the information you've already given in your CV. They are important and should always be treated with respect and filled in with care.

◗◗ COACHING SESSION 50

Filling in the application form

From what you have learned already, what is the key message to remember when you are asked to fill in an application form? Write your answer here.

_____

_____

_____

_____

_____

You should always ensure that any information you give in an application form is **consistent** with information you have given elsewhere, for example in your cover letter and CV. If you don't, you will either have interviewers asking you awkward questions or, worse still, writing you off as someone who isn't telling the truth.

MEETING THE INTERVIEWER

You may be shown into the interview room or the interviewer may come and collect you from wherever you've been waiting. This is an important moment: you have now come face to face with the interviewer for the first time and, because of the impact first impressions make, your fate could be sealed one way or the other in the next few seconds.

If you're seated, get up to shake the interviewer's hand. This is not just to do with politeness: you will make a much better job of shaking hands if you do it from a standing position. Handshakes should be firm and be a 'grasp–shake–release' – holding anyone's hand longer than absolutely necessary is not what most people welcome. Bone-crushing handshakes should definitely be avoided!

The interviewer will normally introduce himself/herself ('Jane Smith. Good morning.') and you should respond in like manner. Look the interviewer in the eye when you introduce yourself but without engaging them in a staring out competition. Most importantly, smile.

FINDING OUT ABOUT THE JOB

Most interviewers will at some point during a preliminary interview take the opportunity to tell you more about:

- the organization
- the job for which you are applying.

You will already have made a list of questions to ask at the interview but you may want to add some notes as the interviewer gives you more information. Ask whether it is OK to do this – not that there could be any objection but it just seems more polite. Taking notes serves two further purposes:

1. It shows that you are listening.
2. After the interview, you might otherwise find yourself struggling to remember everything you have been told.

When the interviewer has finished, you will probably be given the opportunity to ask questions, and here is where you can cast your eye over the questions you prepared in advance and see which points have been covered and which ones haven't.

Don't ask questions about trivial things that have no bearing on your overall view of the job – and that could suggest that you have a skewed sense of priorities. For example, don't ask 'How many days am I allowed to have off sick every year?' Ask only questions about aspects of the job that the interviewer has not covered. If you ask questions about what has already been covered, you will make it obvious that you haven't been listening carefully, which will give a poor impression of you and send out warning signals.

CLOSING THE INTERVIEW

Interviews for the most part run their natural course and you should allow this to happen. Apart from answering the questions you are asked and watching out for those you aren't, your main concern at a preliminary interview is making sure that you have delivered your important messages.

COACHING SESSION 51

Asking closing questions

What would you do if you sensed that an interview was being brought to a close and you hadn't been given the opportunity to ask important questions?

Write your answer here.

_____

_____

_____

_____

_____

_____

Good interviewers will respect your need for information, so, if you are ever put in the position of not being given the chance to ask questions, it is usually a sign that the interviewer is inexperienced. Given that the interview may be your one and only chance to ask questions, you should never go away feeling that you don't know enough about the job to decide whether or not it meets your aspirations. One way of dealing with this situation is to make the point politely that you have some questions you would like to ask and to ask whether now is the right time to do it or whether it would be more convenient if you came back at another time.

Asking what happens next

The interviewer may volunteer the answers to all the questions you have, but, if not, at the end of the interview you should find out the following information:

- How long it will be before you know the outcome of the interview (a rough idea)
- How the outcome will be communicated to you – by letter, email or phone call
- If you have been put forward for the job by an agency, whether you will receive the outcome through them
- Whether there will be a second stage of interviews and, if so, the dates pencilled in for them
- Who will be doing the second interview
- A starting date for the job.

The starting date for most jobs will be determined by the successful candidate's period of notice. Where a member of staff has left or is leaving, the employer's main interest lies in seeing the vacant slot filled as quickly as possible. Some jobs, however, have fixed starting dates. Examples are where the intention is to take on a number of people for the same job (such as a graduate intake) or where a new branch is opening and where, from an induction-training point of view, there will be benefits to everyone starting on the same day.

Asking to know the outcome

Judging by the number of times candidates ask this question in the closing stages of an interview, there must be some 'expert' out there somewhere who thinks it's a good idea to put interviewers on the spot in this way.

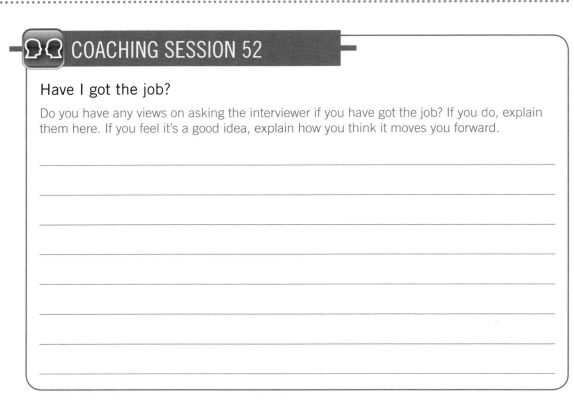

COACHING SESSION 52

Have I got the job?

Do you have any views on asking the interviewer if you have got the job? If you do, explain them here. If you feel it's a good idea, explain how you think it moves you forward.

The idea of asking whether you have got the job is presumably to show the interviewer that you are someone who is good at closing down deals. However, never do this. Interviewers who have heard it all before will simply brush you off with the standard answer that there are other candidates and no decision will be made until they have all been seen.

Inexperienced interviewers may be caught out by the question and find themselves drawn into making ill-thought-out, off-the-cuff remarks about how you performed in the interview. Even someone who is unpractised at interviewing will probably see the dangers of getting into awkward conversations with candidates who haven't impressed, so they avoid the question by equivocating and telling you nothing. The result is that you are none the wiser about how the interview went and nothing has been achieved.

Worse still, though, is where candidates continue to press the point – in some cases going so far as to demand an answer. What such candidates don't appear to appreciate, however, is that by behaving in this way they are sending out a message that they're potentially argumentative and difficult to deal with – that is, the last people in the world an employer would want to get into an employment relationship with. In most cases, it will already have been explained to the candidate that the interview is a preliminary, so asking 'Have I got the job?' suggests that they haven't understood this.

Asking further questions

The closing stages of any interview are just as important as everything that has gone before. As you have seen, it is easy to undo all the work you have done so far by saying something unfortunate at this point.

COACHING SESSION 53

Is there anything you want to add?

Sometimes you are asked this question at the end of an interview and it can have you scratching your head trying to think of something to say. How would you deal with this question?

Write your thoughts down here.

_____

_____

_____

_____

_____

_____

_____

_____

_____

_____

_____

_____

It's a mistake to feel that you need to say something because saying nothing will make you look bad in some way. Succumbing to this feeling could result in you being drawn into talking aimlessly or giving information that is either irrelevant or that the interviewer has heard before. Excursions of this type are sometimes referred to as 'talking yourself out of the job'. It is easy to see why.

Take the view that, if you have succeeded in registering your important messages, there is nothing you will want to add other than your closing statement.

Your closing statement

Sometimes the interviewer will ask you at the end of the interview whether you are interested in the job. Even if you are not asked this question, make a point of saying that:

- you want the job

- you believe you can do it.

During the course of the interview, you may have picked up some negative information about the job that is causing you to have second thoughts. However, unless it is a complete mismatch and you and the interviewer have both agreed that taking it any further is pointless, keep your options open by still saying you want the job. Any final decision to pull out is probably best made away from the interview and when you have had a proper chance to digest everything.

> **!** **COACH'S TIP**
>
> **Remember to say thank you**
>
> It's a common courtesy, when you shake hands with the interviewer to say goodbye, to say thank you for the interview. Not everyone does and interviewers do appreciate it.

FINAL IMPRESSIONS

There are two critical points to any interview. One is at the beginning when first impressions are formed. The other is at the end.

Final impressions are important because these are the impressions interviewers take away with them. Ideally, first and last impressions will be the same and, if you made any faux pas earlier in the interview, this is your chance to take steps to correct them.

There is also a good chance of earlier minor mistakes being overlooked if your final impression confirms a good early impression. This is the halo effect in action.

On the other hand, a faux pas made at the end of an interview will:

- stay fresh in the memory

- occur at the point in the interview furthest removed from the good first impression – and when the halo effect may have worn off slightly.

→ NEXT STEPS

This chapter has been about the challenges you face when you go for a preliminary interview. These challenges are:

- getting your important messages across in the time available

- dealing with interviewers who may not have much insight into what you do for a living

- making sure that you have done enough to stand out from the crowd.

Employers today are cautious when it comes to taking on people. This is partly due to the formidable body of employment protection and human rights legislation that will be in force in most places where this book will be read, which makes it difficult to get rid of people who don't come up to scratch. It is also partly due to the disruptive effect of introducing misfits into teams, particularly if the misfits are people who don't pull their weight or who cause trouble.

What this means in practice is that employers are on high alert to the possibility of bringing in 'bad apples' and, for this reason, candidates need to be extra careful about what they say at interviews. A chance remark is often all it takes, so, when you are being asked questions about why you want to leave your present job, avoid making any statement that could identify you as a potential troublemaker. For example, 'My boss makes unreasonable demands on me' could mean just that, but it is likely to be interpreted as 'I am difficult and awkward and I don't like being given orders.' The play-it-safe interviewer will always conclude the latter.

Finally, you need to remember to be yourself when you go to a preliminary interview and not try to affect personality traits that are alien to you in an attempt to impress the interviewer. This won't work, because your interviewer has got to take a liking to the authentic you. The engagement process has got to start working during the preliminary interview, with people liking you for what you are, not what you are pretending to be.

The next chapter deals with what happens when you get to the next stage. If the preliminary interview went well, you will be among the final few candidates who have been shortlisted and invited back for another showing. The rules of the game are now set to change and you will have new challenges to face.

👍 TAKEAWAYS

Has anything you have read in this chapter caused you to think again about the way you have approached preliminary interviews in the past? Write down here what you will do differently when you are next invited to one.

_____

_____

_____

_____

_____

_____

_____

_____

_____

Have you ever found yourself in the position where you feel the interviewer is rushing you? In hindsight, do you think you could be responsible for the interview running out of time? What action do you plan to take to make sure that this doesn't happen again?

_____

_____

_____

_____

_____

_____

_____

_____

_____

_____

_____

Have you ever come away from an interview feeling that the questions put to you suggest that the interviewer may have a hidden agenda? As a result of reading this chapter, do you feel any better equipped to deal with this situation?

_____

_____

_____

_____

_____

_____

_____

_____

_____

Did you find the section on visual aids helpful? If you haven't done so already, is this an idea you will be taking on board? List any thoughts you have had on what you could include in your visual aids.

_____

_____

_____

_____

_____

_____

_____

_____

_____

_____

_____

_____

Go back to the checklist in coaching session 49. Are there any items that you feel you want to add? List them here.

_____

_____

_____

_____

_____

_____

_____

_____

In your preliminary interviews, are you satisfied that you are managing to get your important messages across or do you find that the opportunity doesn't seem to present itself? What do you think you have learned from reading this chapter that will help you to deliver your important messages?

_____

_____

_____

_____

_____

_____

_____

_____

_____

Have you ever had the experience of coming away from a preliminary interview feeling that you have not been given the chance to ask all the questions about the job you wanted to ask? As a result of reading this chapter, do you feel any better equipped to deal with this situation? What would you do now that you didn't do before?

_____

_____

_____

_____

_____

_____

_____

_____

_____

7 | ON THE SHORTLIST

✔ OUTCOMES FROM THIS CHAPTER

- Understand what it means to be on a shortlist.
- Identify the different challenges you face.
- Recognize the importance of not relaxing your efforts.
- Know what factors influence employers when it comes to making final decisions.

WHAT IT MEANS TO BE ON A SHORTLIST

Being asked to go back for another interview can be taken as a sign that:

- you have passed the test of broad suitability
- everything you have done so far has the employer's seal of approval.

So give yourself a pat on the back but, at the same time, turn your mind to the next set of challenges you face.

💬💬 COACHING SESSION 54

The difference between preliminary and final interviews

List here what you consider to be the most important differences between preliminary interviews and ones where you are in the last few.

1 _____

_____

2 _____

_____

3 _____
_____

4 _____
_____

5 _____
_____

You now have to go through the interview process all over again and, this time, the stakes are higher. Most shortlist interviews are different from preliminary interviews in the following ways:

- You will be dealing with different people – people you haven't met before.

- The test of 'broad suitability' will be replaced by a more stringent test – are you someone the employer will be happy to offer the job to?

- On the plus side, time constraints are usually less of an issue because either longer time slots will be offered to each candidate or they will be seen on separate occasions rather than in succession.

MEETING THE DECISION MAKERS

Sometimes the candidates on the shortlist will be seen again by the same person. This happens where, due to lack of resources, managers with vacancies to fill do their own preliminary interviews and then bring back a few candidates to see again. It is more usual, however, to find that the person who saw you first time round (e.g. the HR manager) hands you on to someone with the responsibility for hiring people in the part of the organization where the job is based. This could be the person who would be your next boss if you were successful, so you now have an opportunity to form a view on whether this is someone you would want to work for.

Second interviews may again be one-on-ones but don't be surprised to find two or more people sitting facing you. A common line-up for a second interview is the line manager with the authority to hire accompanied by either an even more senior person (their boss) or whoever saw you at the first interview, e.g. the HR manager.

Seeing someone different the second time round carries the risk, of course, that they will take an entirely different view of you from the one the first interviewer took.

WHO ELSE IS LEFT IN THE FRAME?

Unless someone tells you, you probably won't know how many other people have been invited back for second interviews and how they compare with you. You can, however, make some fairly safe assumptions.

In terms of the numbers you will be up against, a shortlist interview will be far less formidable than a preliminary interview because some (probably the majority) of the candidates will have been turned down already. You are not therefore confronted with the challenge of making your face stand out from the crowd. However, what you do need to focus your mind on is that the competition at the shortlist stage will consist of people who have impressed in exactly the same way that you have impressed. In other words, from here on, it is all going to get much tougher.

! COACH'S TIP

Don't be complacent

Getting on a shortlist and the good feeling that goes with it can, if you let it, lull you into a false sense of security. However, it's a mistake to feel that you have done the hard part and that the rest will be easy.

👥 COACHING SESSION 55

The cream of the bunch

Given that, like you, the other candidates on the shortlist have also passed the broad test of suitability, what are your thoughts on how to show you are better than them? What in your opinion will persuade the employer to offer the job to you and not to someone else?

Record your answers here.

_____

_____

_____

_____

_____

_____

THE MESSAGES YOU NEED TO GET ACROSS

What you can take as read is that the other candidates on a shortlist will be close to you in terms of what they have to offer. However, there will be differences. In some areas they will be weaker, whereas, in others, they could be streets ahead. What you need to do therefore is get the employer to focus on the areas where you are strongest.

The problem here is that you won't in most cases have any idea of what other candidates have to offer – or what they lack.

What makes you different?

When you are trying to determine what messages you need to get across at a shortlist interview, start by asking yourself whether there is anything in your background that makes you different from most people in your line of work.

- Do you have experience in a field that is unusual for someone who has followed your career path?
- Because of your journey in life, have you picked up some skill or area of expertise that wouldn't normally be found in the occupational group to which you belong?
- Does this experience, skill or area of expertise have relevance to the job for which you are applying?

If it does have relevance, then you could be looking at something that gives you an advantage over the other candidates on the shortlist. This needs to be brought into prominence during the course of the interview.

Your unique selling points

The special attributes you have that set you apart from most other people in your profession are what are known as your unique selling points, or USPs. They are useful weapons to have when:

- you are up against candidates who, in most other respects, are just as good as you
- you need something extra to pinpoint you as the best candidate for the job.

For example, if you have been in the trade or business in question for 25 years, it is a safe bet that you will rate highly against other candidates when it comes to having contacts and knowing your way around. During the second interview, therefore, you can make sure that:

- you mention these facts so that they don't go unnoticed
- you tell the interviewer how you see your experience in the trade as an important asset should you be fortunate enough to get the job.

COACHING SESSION 56

List your USPs

Is there anything in your portfolio that marks you out as different from other people you know in your line of work?

List here any unique selling points you think you have.

1 _____

_____

_____

2 _____

_____

_____

3 _____

_____

_____

4 _____

_____

_____

5 _____

_____

_____

COACH'S TIP

Use your USP

Get your USP on to the agenda so that you can plant the idea in the interviewer's head that what marks you out as different is (a) important and (b) should be given a high ranking in the selection criteria.

KEEPING UP THE GOOD WORK

What getting on to a shortlist does mean is that you made a good job of the first interview and that someone saw something in you that they took a liking to. What would help, of course, would be knowledge of what that something was.

COACHING SESSION 57

Looking for clues

Imagine you have been put on a shortlist for a job and you want to find out what impressed the interviewer at the first interview. Where do you look for clues?

Write down your ideas here.

_____

_____

_____

_____

_____

_____

Feedback from the interviewer

Some interviewers may be helpful when it comes to giving feedback from the preliminary interview. They may even, at the end of that interview, share their thoughts with the candidate about what they see as their good points and weak points. Such helpfulness is, however, rare, for the following reasons:

- Interviewers are understandably nervous about raising people's expectations when there are still other candidates to see.

- Where the feedback is negative, there is always the potential for the discussion to become acrimonious.

There are different schools of thought on the merits of phoning up the interviewer who put you on the shortlist and asking for feedback. You may get someone who is willing to be helpful; on the other hand, you may learn nothing useful and, at the same time, run the risk that the interviewer may not welcome being quizzed in this way. At a stroke, you could undo all the good work you have done.

Clues from the preliminary interview

The way the discussion went at the first interview, the questions that were asked and the amount of time spent on specific areas of your portfolio all offer clues about where the interviewer's interests lay. You also have the advantage of having listened to the interviewer talking about the job itself, which will give you further clues about your suitability. If you asked the first interviewer for their view on the important qualities needed, you will have added further to your fund of useful knowledge.

Feedback from recruitment consultants

Where you have been put forward for the job by a firm of recruitment consultants (an agency), the consultant will usually make it his or her business to ring the interviewer and ask for some feedback. Some interviewers may be cagey with the answers they give to consultants unless the feedback is good. Because employers and recruitment consultants often have relationships going back over many years, there is a level of openness in the conversations that go on between them that wouldn't be the case if you phoned the interviewer direct.

WHAT INFLUENCES THE OUTCOME

A shortlist interview is very much a case of carrying on where the first interview left off. You have done well up to now, so you need keep going. Focus on what got you this far and see to it that you give the employer more of the same.

Having said this, the outcome of shortlist interviews still relies to a large degree on subjective judgements. You got on well with the first interviewer and, on the strength of this, you found yourself with a place on the shortlist. However, it doesn't necessarily follow that you will establish the same rapport with the second interviewer. The engagement process has to start all over again.

FINE LINES AND CLOSE CALLS

When candidates are closely matched it is not unusual to find that, at the end of a series of interviews and re-interviews, a number of them are perfectly capable of doing the job. What do employers do in such situations? There is only one job, so somehow they have got to decide whom to offer it to and whom to turn down.

COACHING SESSION 58

The final choice

Put yourself in the shoes of an employer faced with the decision of having to choose between two excellent candidates. How would you proceed?

Write your thoughts down here.

_____

_____

_____

_____

_____

_____

_____

_____

_____

_____

_____

_____

_____

_____

_____

_____

_____

It is unlikely that the decision about whom to appoint will be so close as to be a matter of flipping a coin, but making a choice between two evenly matched candidates can turn on what may otherwise be seen as fairly minor points. Often, the alternative in these situations is to bring both candidates back and give them another showing, so, if you find yourself being asked to go in again after what you thought was the final interview, this might be because you are neck and neck with another candidate.

Integrity is a big issue when it comes to these close calls and it is important not to do anything at an interview that could put a dent in your credibility, however minor. An example of this is carelessly saying something during the interview that contradicts information you have given in your CV or application form.

> **! COACH'S TIP**
>
> ## Keep your credibility
>
> If you are called back once more for another second interview, you still have a job to do. Take care again that you don't, by some slip of the tongue, contradict information you gave at the earlier interview.

→ NEXT STEPS

This chapter has looked at the different challenges you face when you are on the shortlist for a job and among the last few candidates. The key points are as follows:

- The candidates you are up against will, in many cases, be every bit as good as you.
- Employers think differently when they have to make their minds up about who gets the job.

Your challenge, then, is to:

- prove that you have more to offer than other candidates by taking every opportunity to bring into the discussion your strongest points
- convince employers that, if they take you on, you will be an asset to their business.

Bringing a new face into an organization is a big step and employers are mindful of the fact that making a bad choice can have serious consequences for them. They will not only have the difficulty of exiting the bad choice (a potentially costly process) but will also have to face up to repairing the damage that the bad choice has caused. For these reasons, employers tend to play safe and proceed with caution when it comes to making final selection decisions. Where there are doubts about a candidate – particularly doubts about his or her character and personal integrity – then their instincts will tell them not to take the risk. An unfortunate remark at an interview is often all it takes to sow a seed of doubt and nowhere more so than at a shortlist interview. At this stage, interviewers will be:

- aware that they are at the stage where they have to make a final decision
- on high alert, for this reason, for picking up all areas of doubt
- tending to go on for longer so that there is a greater risk of candidates relaxing their guard and saying something that lets them down.

The next chapter takes you away from the world of interviews for jobs that are competitively fought over and into the elusive invisible market. Here, the challenges you face when you go for an interview are different and different rules apply.

👍 TAKEAWAYS

As a result of reading this chapter, have you changed your opinion about the nature of the competition you will face when you get on a shortlist? How has your opinion changed?

_____

_____

_____

_____

_____

_____

_____

_____

_____

Did you find the advice about focusing on what makes you different helpful? Will it change the way you approach shortlist interviews?

_____

_____

_____

_____

_____

_____

_____

_____

_____

_____

_____

_____

Did the section on keeping up the good work make you think? What points for action did you come up with after reading this section? Note them here.

_____

_____

_____

_____

_____

_____

_____

_____

When you're called back for another interview, do you think you can do any better to ensure that your credibility remains intact? Make a note here of any thoughts that crossed your mind.

_____

_____

_____

_____

_____

_____

_____

_____

_____

_____

Looking back to the last time you attended a shortlist interview, is there anything you would now do differently?

_____

_____

_____

_____

_____

_____

_____

_____

_____

_____

_____

_____

_____

_____

_____

_____

_____

_____

_____

_____

_____

_____

_____

_____

_____

ONLINE RESOURCE

Not getting on to shortlists

To find out more about why people don't get on to shortlists, access the free download. Go to the following website:

www.TYCoachbooks.com/Interviews

INTERVIEWS THROUGH PROACTIVE SOURCING

OUTCOMES FROM THIS CHAPTER

- Know about the invisible job market and what defines it.
- Understand what proactive sourcing means.
- Realize how interviews for jobs sourced proactively differ from those for jobs sourced by other means.
- Know what challenges you face when you go for an interview that has been sourced proactively and how to deal with them.

THE INVISIBLE JOB MARKET

The **invisible** job market is a term used to describe the market for jobs that aren't advertised: jobs that, for one reason or another, employers prefer to keep to themselves. Conversely, the **visible** market refers to jobs that are advertised and that are there for everyone to see.

🗩🗩 COACHING SESSION 59

Accessing the invisible market

Can you think of ways of accessing the invisible job market?

Write them down here.

1 _____

_____

_____

_____

2 _____

_____

_____

_____

3 _____

_____

_____

_____

4 _____

_____

_____

_____

5 _____

_____

_____

_____

_____

There are a number of methods you can use to access the invisible job market. The three main ones are:

1. **Making unsolicited approaches to employers:** ringing them up or sending out mailshots in much the same way that Scott sent out a mailshot to his firm's leading competitors in Chapter 2

2. **Professional networking:** putting the word round among people you're connected with through your work

3. **Registering with recruitment consultants (agencies):** getting consultants to do the sourcing for you.

Proactive sourcing is the collective term used to describe all these methods of accessing the invisible job market. Proactive sourcing is where the stimulus comes from you. Reactive sourcing, on the other hand, is where the stimulus comes from the employer, usually in the form of advertising. Reactive sourcing is therefore used to access the visible market.

COACHING SESSION 60

The unsolicited approach

To illustrate how this might work, consider the following case study.

Case study: Sam and Lou

Sam is the Chief Executive of a fast-growing distribution business who has just seen his logistics manager walk out on him at short notice. Sam is now considering his options. What he can't afford to do is to leave the logistics manager's job open for too long because, if he does, it will soon start to have a serious impact on the performance of the business.

At this point, Sam remembers an unsolicited CV that arrived in the post two months earlier. The CV was from someone named Lou who was enquiring to see whether there were any opportunities for logistics managers. Sam had no vacancies at the time, so he wrote back to Lou explaining the position, thanking him for his interest and saying that he would keep the CV on file. Sam now retrieves Lou's CV from the file where he put it and reads it again. It looks promising, he tells himself – and, if Lou proved suitable, it would save the time and trouble of advertising the job, then having to trawl through dozens of applicants. With these thoughts in mind, Sam decides to ask Lou to come in for an interview.

What important differences will there be between the interview Sam is planning to have with Lou – an unadvertised job – and the kind of interview you would have for a job you have seen advertised? Write your thoughts down in the table below.

An unadvertised job	An advertised job

THE ADVANTAGES OF PROACTIVE SOURCING

Serious job-hunters, take note: sourcing jobs on the invisible market has several major advantages. The main one is that there is little or no competition to consider. While sending out mailshots and cold-calling employers may sometimes seem like a lot of effort for little result, it can and does work.

The lack of competition

In the case study above, Sam is hoping to get a key position that has become vacant filled as quickly as he can. Lou may or may not be the right person for the job. If he is, though – and the signs are good – it will save Sam the trouble of having to go through a complex recruitment exercise.

From Lou's point of view, what's interesting about this interview is that no one else is being seen (not that he knows this yet). In effect, he is the only runner in a one-horse race, so, unless he has the bad luck to fall at one of the fences, he is going to be the winner. Contrast this with the kind of interviews that come your way as a result of applying for jobs you have seen advertised (reactive sourcing). Here, unless you happen to have a set of highly in-demand skills, you will probably find you're up against candidates who number in double figures.

Having the interviewer predisposed towards you

Another feature of the interview that Lou is about to have with Sam is that Sam (the interviewer) will want the interview to go well. If Lou does tick all the boxes, then it will save Sam a lot of time and trouble. Sam will therefore be more inclined to gloss over minor blemishes in Lou's track record and will be keen to get on with the job of getting him started. The same could not be said about an interview for a job where you are one of many applicants and where the purpose of the interview will be to sort the wheat from the chaff. Any minor blemishes would be quickly picked up.

! COACH'S TIP

'The job is yours.'

An interview where you are the only applicant has more chance of ending with the job being offered to you than one where other candidates are in the frame.

COACHING SESSION 61

Sparking interest

Sam is a man in a hurry, but can you think of any other situations where an unsolicited CV landing on someone's desk might spark off interest? Write your answers here.

_____

_____

_____

_____

_____

_____

The lack of job specification

This might seem at first glance to be a disadvantage. When Sam speaks to Lou on the phone he may tell Lou why he wants to see him, but, in many cases, when you go for an interview you have sourced proactively, you will be walking in blind. Scott in Chapter 2 was a good example. He went to his interview with no clear idea of what the job would be at the end of it. What this means, of course, is that, without knowing what the employer is looking for, it is hard or impossible to know:

- what you have to offer that will interest the employer
- as a consequence, what your important messages are.

However, Scott is also a good example of someone who might tempt an employer in the same line of business to create a slot for him. He comes with a good sales track record and any competitor reading his CV would see straight away the potential for hiring someone who would bring in business. Another example of an employer creating a slot just for you is where you have a lot of know-how locked in your head – know-how an employer would be keen to acquire.

Jobs that are on hold

A phenomenon of recessionary times is that, instead of replacing people who leave, employers put vacancies on hold, waiting perhaps for the green shoots of recovery to appear or some other favourable sign that would make them feel more confident about hiring. An interesting-looking CV landing on someone's desk at such a time might just tempt an employer at least to take a look at the person who has sent it in.

COACHING SESSION 62

Using a recruitment consultant

Here is another case study for you to consider – about sourcing a job through an agency.

Case study: Sal

Sal works in HR for a large retail group where she has been employed for six-and-a-half years. When she first got the job she was grateful for the opportunity it gave her to break into her chosen career. Now, however, she feels that the time has come to make a move. She is set on joining an organization that will be able to offer her better prospects and the chance to advance up the ladder into a management position.

Six weeks earlier, Sal registered with a firm of recruitment consultants specializing in HR appointments. One evening she receives a call at home from a consultant named Jas, who wants to speak to her about a position with a firm of electrical goods retailers that seems to be right up her street.

Jas explains that everything is hush-hush at the moment because the present incumbent of the position is someone who hasn't come up to expectations but has not yet been told. The main purpose of Jas's call is to see whether Sal can attend an off-site interview with the firm's HR director. Sal asks a few questions about the position, in reply to which Jas paints a rosy picture indicating a good starting salary, an attractive package of fringe benefits and the possibility of promotion in a year's time to a more senior role at the firm's head office.

Sal asks whether she is the only candidate the agency is putting forward for the position. Jas confirms that she is; the HR director looked through a number of CVs but Sal's is the only one he picked out.

1. What is your reading of this case study?

   _____

   _____

   _____

   _____

   _____

2. If you were Sal, how reliable would you find the information that there are no other candidates for the position?

   _____

   _____

   _____

   _____

   _____

3. As a consequence, how would you treat the interview with the HR director?

_____

_____

_____

_____

_____

4. In what way would a consultant like Jas be able to help you prepare for the interview?

_____

_____

_____

_____

_____

What Sal doesn't know is whether or not the firm of electrical goods retailers has been in touch with other recruitment consultants besides the organization Jas works for. If it has, there may well be other candidates in the frame. For this reason, it would be sensible to treat the interview much like any other. It is also possible that Jas has told Sal that she is the only candidate just to encourage her to go to the interview. Jas, after all, has a vested interest in seeing her get the job because of the commission he would earn.

On the plus side, however, Jas has probably been given an indication of what attributes the firm is seeking in candidates for the position. By asking him the right questions, Sal could find out what the requirements are and use this information to pinpoint the main messages she needs to get across at the interview. The interview is not therefore as 'blind' as most interviews Sal would get by proactive sourcing.

PROFESSIONAL NETWORKING

Tapping into your contacts is a very effective way of getting interviews. The success people have with networking their way into jobs emphasizes again the importance of comfort factors when employers are faced with the decision of hiring people. Someone who comes with a recommendation from a trusted source will stand streets ahead of someone who is a completely unknown quantity.

COACHING SESSION 63

The networking approach

Here is a case study describing the experience of someone sourcing an interview through professional networking.

Case study: Richard

Richard has heard on the grapevine that the office where he works could be closing in six months' time. Richard has been made redundant several times before and he knows how it makes sense, when rumours like these start, to get as many irons in the fire as possible. With this in mind, he starts scanning the ads in the press and on websites and registering with a few firms of recruitment consultants. In addition, Richard spreads the word among some of his former work colleagues who have now moved on to other organizations. One of these former colleagues is Abi who, a few days later, rings him to say that she mentioned his situation to her boss and now her boss wants to interview him. Richard asks Abi whether she knows any more, but she replies that she doesn't.

1. What are your thoughts on this case study?

_____

_____

_____

_____

_____

_____

2. In what ways would the interview with Abi's boss be different from most other interviews?

_____

_____

_____

_____

_____

_____

_____

Regrettably, most people only think of using professional networking as a way of accessing opportunities when they have their backs to the wall – when, like Richard, they are facing redundancy or when some other catastrophe is about to descend on them. However, they are an important way of accessing the invisible job market whatever your position may be.

What's different about interviews you source by professional networking? Using Richard as the example, it's safe to assume that Abi has put in a good word for him. Abi's boss has been given what amounts to a personal recommendation. This isn't a guarantee that Richard will be offered a job, but it is a clear sign that:

- Abi's boss holds her in high regard
- anyone recommended by Abi should be taken seriously
- Richard's lifelong interview has worked for him.

When the interview is with someone you know

Sourcing interviews by professional networking may also lead to a situation where the person interviewing you is someone you know. For example, your old boss with whom you had a good relationship has moved on and is now working somewhere else. You, for whatever reason, make contact with your old boss to explore the possibility of employment and the result is an interview.

COACHING SESSION 64

What they know about you

Imagine you're in the position of going for an interview with a former boss or work colleague. Apart from chatting about old times, what, in your opinion, will be (a) different about the interview and (b) different about the challenges you face?

Write your answers below.

_____

_____

_____

_____

_____

_____

_____

Here is where you will be putting your lifelong interview to the test. When the interviewer already knows you, the examination of your competence, experience and general character that forms the greater part of most interviews won't be such an issue. The interviewer will know what you have to offer but, at the same time, he or she will also know your flaws. For example, when the two of you last worked together you may have made a few mistakes. If so, you can expect questions about what you've done to mend your ways. The interviewer could even ask you to convince him or her that, given the offer of a job, you won't go back to your old habits. What you thought was going to be a walkover turns out not to be the case.

🗩🗩 COACHING SESSION 65

Increasing the comfort factors

Imagine that you're at an interview with someone who was once your immediate boss in a previous job. At that time, you were going through a bad spell following the break-up of a long-term relationship. This culminated in a period when you lost a lot of time from work due to unexplained absences and which resulted in you receiving a number of warnings.

Incorporating the lessons from earlier chapters about employers needing to feel comfortable with the answers you give, what would you say to make your old boss feel happy that you've turned over a new leaf?

1. Write your answers here.

_____

_____

_____

_____

_____

2. Now put yourself in your old boss's shoes and look back at the answer you have given. Is there anything you've said that might still leave your old boss feeling uncomfortable? If so, how can you improve your answer?

_____

_____

_____

_____

_____

HANDLING PROACTIVELY SOURCED INTERVIEWS

In Chapter 2 in the case of Scott, you saw the importance of making your aspirations clear in your cover letter and CV. You should equally make your aspirations clear when you are:

- registering with firms of recruitment consultants
- putting the word round to your professional contacts.

The penalty for not doing this (as you saw in Scott's case) is being invited to attend interviews that are time-wasters. While this may not matter so much if you are out of work, it could have an enormous impact on your capacity to go to interviews if you can't get the time off without raising a few eyebrows.

No fixed agenda

An unsolicited approach like Scott's could also result in an employer agreeing to see you with no fixed ideas about what the potential outcome might be. At some appropriate point in the interview – unless it has been made clear already – it would therefore be advisable to ask the interviewer whether he or she has anything specific in mind. In this way, you will be able to form a view about whether the interview is leading anywhere or not.

Fishing expeditions

Again, Scott's case is a good example. Employers sometimes ask submitters of unsolicited CVs to come in for an interview for no other reason than to meet someone working in the same business sector. Sometimes, however, the motives for these friendly chats are not as innocent as they seem: while it is unlikely that Scott would be asked to provide details of his ten top customers and his firm's pricing policies, he might find himself facing some mild pumping about matters that are commercially sensitive. He will need to fend off this pumping or he could find himself in hot water if it ever got back to his employer's ears.

COACHING SESSION 66

When they are not hiring

Imagine that, in response to sending an unsolicited CV, you've been invited to an interview where the interviewer (a senior executive in the business) asks you a lot of questions before eventually revealing that there *might* be a vacancy for someone like you at some point in the near future. You ask him to explain, but his replies are cagey. He talks about the business 'flatlining' and how he will have to give it careful thought before hiring anyone.

Ten days later you get a letter from the interviewer to say that, after giving the matter a lot of thought and talking it over with his colleagues, he has decided to shelve any recruitment plans for the time being. He promises to keep your details on file and asks you to let him know if your circumstances change. The letter ends with the usual polite thank-yous and best wishes.

1. How do you read this situation? Is this someone stringing you along and giving you false hopes or someone who is genuine and acting responsibly in the face of unfavourable business conditions?

2. What do you do now? Can you think of any action you should be taking to keep your chances of getting the job alive? Alternatively, do you do nothing and write it off to experience?

MANAGING PROACTIVELY SOURCED INTERVIEWS

As you have seen, in recessionary times employers often put their recruitment plans on hold. Then an interesting CV arrives in the post or by email and the employer feels tempted to see the individual who has sent it in. Sometimes, this works in the candidate's favour. Employers like what they see and push to one side any concerns as to whether this is the right time to hire or not. Sometimes, however, situations arise like the one described above.

What is difficult or impossible to judge is whether the job will surface again at some point in the future or whether the employer simply didn't like you and used the excuse of putting the job on hold as a way of letting you down gently.

At this point, it's important to do nothing that could spoil your chances. While you might be tempted to write a not-too-polite letter back asking the employer to reimburse your travelling expenses, it would be better by far to take the following steps:

1. Write a letter or email thanking the interviewer for seeing you and expressing your interest in the job should it ever become available.

2. Count off six weeks and write to the interviewer again:
    a) to remind him who you are
    b) to ask whether anything has changed
    c) to say that you are still interested in the job.

3. Repeat this exercise every so often.

This process is about maintaining your **visibility**, which is one of the subjects you will be learning more about in Chapter 10.

! COACH'S TIP

Keep your face in the frame

Keeping your face in the frame when an employer can't decide whether to hire or not is a good example of visibility. It can and does pay off and, with a job that you have proactively sourced, you are still in the enviable position of being there first – before the competition arrives.

→ NEXT STEPS

This chapter has been about an area of the job market that may not be familiar to you because so far in life you may have made all your job moves by replying to advertisements – the visible market. When you go for an interview that you have sourced proactively – when, for example, you send out a batch of unsolicited CVs to employers on a mailing list you have compiled – you face rather different challenges. Competition is rarely an issue with proactively sourced interviews, but there are other challenges, which are:

- being able to talk persuasively to employers who may be hesitant about hiring

- being prepared for what might be a long hard slog post-interview, before you land the job

- being ready for the interview ending with a job offer and knowing how you would respond.

Where you have sourced the interview by networking, an additional challenge includes talking to employers who already have insights into your character, work ethic and ability, which wouldn't be the case with employers who have no previous knowledge of you. You will have to be ready for any tricky questions that might ensue.

The next chapter looks at what happens after an interview, when:

- the outcome of an interview is not favourable

- what you can do about it.

👍 TAKEAWAYS

As a result of reading this chapter, have you changed your mind about how to handle proactively sourced interviews? Say in what ways your mind has changed.

_____

_____

_____

_____

_____

_____

_____

_____

_____

Have you changed your expectations of what a proactively sourced interview could lead to? In what ways? Do you rate the chances of a proactively sourced interview landing you a good job higher, lower or about the same as you did previously?

_____

_____

_____

_____

_____

_____

_____

_____

_____

_____

_____

Do you plan to make any changes to the way in which you prepare for proactively sourced interviews? Write down any information that you found particularly useful.

_____

_____

_____

_____

_____

_____

_____

_____

_____

_____

Do you plan to make any changes to the way you approach interviews with interviewers who know you or who know you through shared acquaintances? If you do, what do you plan to do differently?

_____

_____

_____

_____

_____

_____

_____

_____

_____

_____

_____

Have you learned anything new about how to deal with recruitment consultants (agencies)? List here what you consider to be the most important points.

_____

_____

_____

_____

_____

_____

_____

_____

_____

As a result of reading this chapter, do you feel more equipped to deal with interviews that don't appear to be going anywhere? Make a list of any points that struck you as particularly important.

_____

_____

_____

_____

_____

_____

_____

_____

_____

_____

Has reading this chapter encouraged you to do more to source jobs by using proactive methods? Have you devised any plans and, if so, what are they?

_____

_____

_____

_____

_____

_____

_____

_____

_____

_____

_____

_____

9 AFTER INTERVIEWS

✔ OUTCOMES FROM THIS CHAPTER

- Know how to rate your chances of success after an interview.
- Know what to read into it when you're not offered the job.
- Understand the importance of not doing anything that might spoil your chances of success.

'HOW DID I DO?'

This is a question all interview candidates ask themselves. 'How do I think my interview went?' 'What are my chances of getting the job?'

🗩🗩 COACHING SESSION 67

Interpreting the signs

Here is another case study for you to consider.

Case study: Dev

Dev applied for a position as an IT manager and he has recently been for a second interview. The interview went well in his opinion and he is confident of the outcome. In fact, as the interview came to a close, the interviewer made a point of telling Dev that he had made a favourable impression and stood a good chance of getting the job. Another encouraging sign, in Dev's view, was that the interview lasted over two hours. Dev reckoned that the interviewer would not have spent so much time with him unless he was seriously interested.

1. What is your reading of this case study? Is Dev right to be building up his hopes?

_____

_____

_____

_____

_____

_____

2. What other explanation can you give for the interviewer's encouraging remarks and the length of time the interview took? Write your thoughts down here.

_____

_____

_____

_____

_____

False readings

Perhaps the most striking thing to note about the readings candidates make of their own interview performance is how often they get it wrong. They think that they've done well and then find that they're not offered the job but they can't work out why. Why is it so easy to make false readings? Go through this short checklist to help you to understand how this can happen.

■ **The interviewer was warm and friendly.**

Candidates have a tendency to judge interviews in terms of how well they got on with the interviewer. Their optimism in many cases is based on nothing more than feeling that they hit it off with the person who sat on the other side of the desk. Good interviewers are, of course, skilled at putting candidates at their ease. Their friendliness is part of their expertise and not necessarily a sign that they've taken a shine to someone.

■ **The interviewer was encouraging about your chances.**

As Dev found, some interviewers make encouraging remarks to candidates and even go so far as to suggest that they stand a good chance of getting the job. Always take remarks such as these with a pinch of salt. It is usually a sign that the interviewer is inexperienced. It is also common to find that they make remarks like this to everyone.

- **The interview was lengthy.**

Like Dev, candidates often judge interviews by their length. They see a long interview as a good sign and one that lasts only 20 minutes as a sign that the interviewer took an instant dislike to them. While it is true that busy interviewers don't waste time on people they view as no-hopers, the length of an interview is often more to do with the interviewer's style than anything else. Some interviewers do always spend hours with candidates.

- **You are a great match for the job.**

Candidates feel they have done well if they have demonstrated that they can do the job. They forget there are other criteria involved in selection, such as whether they would 'fit in' or not. They also forget that there will be other candidates who are equally capable of doing the job.

The problem of raised expectations

Candidates can start to feel disgruntled when they get the letter turning them down. 'I could have done the job with my eyes closed,' you hear them saying. They end up blaming the interviewer. Finding that you've built up your hopes only to have them dashed tends to lead not just to disappointment but, in some cases, to anger, too. There will be more on the subject of anger later in the chapter.

> **! COACH'S TIP**
>
> Don't dwell on it
>
> After you have been for an interview, it is quite natural to think about it but, as far as you can, leave it at that. View the outcome as something that could go either way.

WHAT TO DO WHEN YOU'RE NOT OFFERED THE JOB

Irrespective of whether you've managed to keep your expectations in check or not, the news that you've not got the job always comes as a big disappointment. It is an even bigger disappointment when you've got as far as being put on a shortlist. Your thoughts tend to turn to these questions:

- Who did get the job?
- What more did they have to offer than me?

COACHING SESSION 68

Trying to get feedback

1. Do you think it is worth phoning the interviewer to ask why you didn't get the job? Do you have any experience of doing this and, if so, what did you learn?

_____

_____

_____

_____

_____

_____

2. Did you find it useful?

_____

_____

_____

_____

_____

_____

The subject of getting feedback from interviewers has been touched on already in the context of preliminary interviews that have gone well and trying to find out what they liked about you (what you need to keep plugging at the second interview). But when you've been turned down for the job, what is there to lose? If it means that you cause someone irritation, so what?

As with that earlier situation, it is advisable to think twice about phoning interviewers and asking for feedback, for the following reasons:

- Unless you're lucky, the feedback may not be helpful.

- The interviewers may not take kindly to being quizzed in this way and you could end up undoing all the good work you have done.

- These conversations can become acrimonious. Something is said that leads you to challenge the decision that has been made about you.

COACHING SESSION 69

The show's not over yet

Can you think of any reason why it's a good idea to stay on the right side of employers who turn you down after a final interview?

Write your answer here:

_____

_____

_____

_____

_____

_____

_____

_____

_____

_____

_____

_____

Getting on a shortlist is evidence in itself that you've passed the test of broad suitability and managed successfully to get into the last few. It is reasonably safe to assume therefore that you have made a good impression on someone or possibly on a number of people. You didn't get the job but it is probable that the final decision was a close call, with not much between you and the candidate who was successful. But now consider two further possibilities:

1. The candidate who got the job decides to turn the offer down.

2. In the near future, another vacancy arises with the same employer and, before advertising the position, they decide to look back at previous candidates.

Here is where asking the interviewer why you didn't get the job and running the risk of annoying them would definitely not be in your best interests. Later in the chapter, there is more on what you can do when you're the runner-up.

Empty gestures

Some candidates have adopted the practice of waiting for the turn-down letter to drop on the doormat or into their email inbox before sending in their bill for travel expenses and other costs they incurred in getting to the interviews. The common form of such demands is curt and the reason for sending them has more to do with pique than hardship. Again, all the good work these candidates have done is wiped out at a stroke.

! COACH'S TIP

Don't ruin your future chances

Try not to give way to feelings of anger when you don't get the job. The story may not be over yet and you want to keep on the right side of employers who have taken a positive view of you. You should therefore never do anything that could queer the pitch.

Looking for feedback

Helpful feedback on why you didn't get the job is usually in short supply, so trying to work out where you went wrong and what you need to do to put it right is largely wasted effort. The only exception, perhaps, is where you have been put forward for the job by a firm of recruitment consultants. Recruitment consultants have their eyes firmly fixed on the commissions they earn from making successful placements, so they are usually anxious to find out as much as possible about how a programme of final interviews went. Employers will often tell them why a candidate they've put forward hasn't been successful, though the amount of detail they go into varies enormously.

How much of this information gets passed back to the candidate is another matter. Just like employers, consultants are mindful of getting drawn into acrimonious discussions with candidates or, worse still, finding that candidates who don't like what they're being told or who feel that the judgement of them is unfair vent their feelings by ringing up the employers concerned. Needless to say, employers put in this position won't be happy about it and it may even cause them to prevent any more business being placed with the consultants. This is why, even where a firm of recruitment consultants have been involved, your quest to find out where you went wrong may result in you receiving nothing more than a few unhelpful platitudes.

COACHING SESSION 70

The less said the better

Apart from not wanting to get drawn into acrimonious discussions, can you think of any other reason why employers are reluctant to furnish candidates with details of why they didn't get the job?

Write your answer here.

_____

_____

_____

_____

_____

_____

_____

_____

Employers today are increasingly the target for litigation, so they will be careful not to say anything that could provide someone with the ammunition they need to bring a claim. 'The less said the better' is the ground rule most employers stick to, and who can blame them?

Looking for clues

Racking your brains over where you went wrong and what you need to do to put it right is a futile exercise in the context of one interview. Subjectivity alone means that any conclusion you come to will have little validity unless viewed across a wider spectrum of interviews. But if you keep getting on to shortlists and then finding you go no further, there may be an explanation – something you can put right. Bear in mind, though, that what you're looking for is going to be something fairly minor. Anything any bigger would have meant that you didn't get on the shortlist in the first place.

Don't change your tactics

Getting on to shortlists – particularly where jobs have had exposure on the visible or advertised market – is a sign that your approach is working, so changing it might be a mistake. More important by far is to keep going. Sooner or later, you will connect with the right opportunity.

WHAT TO DO WHEN YOU'RE A RUNNER-UP

Successful candidates don't always accept the offers made to them or, when they tell their employers they've been offered another job, they find inducements placed in front of them to persuade them to stay.

What do employers do when they find the candidate they offered the job to lets them down?

Back to square one

The thought of having to go back and start the selection process again won't be appealing, so many employers in this situation will start by looking back over the shortlist. Was there an acceptable number two? Providing number two has done nothing to spoil their chances, they might find they get a phone call they didn't expect.

This may seem obvious, but employers don't always do the obvious, for the following reasons:

- It doesn't occur to them.

- They've already turned down number two and they would find it too hard to go back to them with an offer.

- Since the number two now knows he or she wasn't the first choice, some employers will feel that this would be a bad start.

- Employers assume the number two won't be interested either, either because of being turned down once or because of the passage of time.

The readvertisement

A candidate who has been turned down for a job may be surprised to find that, a few weeks later, it is being advertised again. Should they apply? Most candidates take the view that there's no point. They've been turned down once so the likelihood is they'll be turned down again.

COACHING SESSION 71

The job comes up again

There's a job standing vacant that interested you a short while ago and that you almost got but now it has become available again. Do you have any thoughts on how you could capitalize on this situation? What, if anything, do you do?

Write your answer here.

_____

_____

_____

_____

_____

_____

_____

_____

_____

_____

_____

_____

_____

_____

_____

_____

> ## ❗ COACH'S TIP
>
> ### Get in before the competition arrives
>
> Unfortunately, once the job has gone back on to the open (visible) market, it will attract competition again. So, if you're going to gain any advantage from being one of the runners-up first time round, you ideally need to act before the employer starts placing ads and contacting recruitment consultants.

Maintaining visibility

Here's what to do when you don't get a job after being put on a shortlist.

When you get the turn-down letter, count off five working days and then write a polite letter back saying how disappointed you were to hear that you didn't get the job but thanking the employer for the interviews and expressing your continuing interest if a similar opportunity should ever arise in the future. Not many, if any, of the other unsuccessful candidates will have done the same, so you immediately stand out. The association in the employer's mind will be with someone who can take the disappointment on the chin and still come up smiling – a good association.

Wait four weeks, and then email the employer. Remind them who you are (this is important) and then ask them whether they managed to fill the position. Explain that you emailed on the off chance that they might still be looking for someone. Say that you were very interested in the position and disappointed when you didn't get it, etc.

The timing of this email is aimed at coinciding with two possible events:

- The selected candidate didn't start and the employer is in a spin about what to do next.

- The selected candidate did start but it has already become apparent to the employer that they made the wrong choice.

- Any barriers the employer may have felt about making contact with you again have now been demolished (by you). You're there. You're ready and waiting for them to start talking to you again.

The above is an exercise in **visibility,** or being in the right place at the right time.

→ NEXT STEPS

Being good at interviews extends beyond the interview itself. Going there on the day and giving it your best shot is one thing, but you also have to manage the outcomes, whatever they may be, including outcomes where the decisions haven't gone in your favour.

If you have been brought back for two or more interviews, you have succeeded in sparking interest. You may not have been offered the job this time round, but who knows what the future may hold? Indeed, there are cases of candidates who have been seen as 'too good for the job' and who have been contacted again months (and, in some cases, years) later when another, far better position has arisen.

This chapter about life after interviews has highlighted:

- the dangers of raising your expectations to heights that will be difficult to come down from if the offer of the job doesn't come your way

- the benefits for you in keeping the lines open to employers who have rejected you after you reached the shortlist stage

- the emptiness of gestures that have no purpose other than to retaliate against employers who have turned you down – gestures such as putting in a claim for expenses.

Everything you have learned in this chapter is relevant to the next one, which considers the issues facing you when the offer of a job is put in your hands and you have to decide whether to accept it or not.

👍 TAKEAWAYS

As a result of reading this chapter, will you be doing anything differently to manage your expectations after you've been for an interview? What will you be doing now that you haven't done previously?

_____

_____

_____

_____

_____

_____

_____

_____

_____

Have you learned anything useful about managing the disappointment of being turned down for a job? What are the most important lessons you have learned?

_____

_____

_____

_____

_____

_____

_____

_____

_____

_____

_____

What did the section on what you can do when you're a runner-up make you think? Is it advice you will follow?

_____

_____

_____

_____

_____

_____

_____

_____

_____

What have you learned about always taking the positives from the outcomes of job applications, even though they may not have been the ones you wanted?

_____

_____

_____

_____

_____

_____

_____

_____

_____

In the past, do you think you may have done anything to queer the pitch with employers who have turned you down? Do you now see this as a mistake? If so, what will you be doing to ensure that you don't make this mistake again?

_____

_____

_____

_____

_____

_____

_____

_____

_____

Write down a strategy for how you can maintain your visibility with an employer even after you have been turned down after a second interview.

_____

_____

_____

_____

_____

_____

_____

_____

_____

_____

_____

_____

_____

10 | GETTING THE JOB

✔ OUTCOMES FROM THIS CHAPTER

- Know how to approach the decision about whether to accept an offer.
- Understand how to consider the risks.
- Know what to do when a job offer falls short of your expectations.
- Recognize a bad move and know how to avoid making one.
- Know what to do when you've made up your mind to accept an offer.

DECIDING TO CHANGE JOBS

What's good about going to interviews is that you get to meet employers face to face. Most importantly, you get to meet the person who could be your next boss and the way the meeting went will tell you a great deal about whether or not this is someone you would get along with. Yet a job move is still largely a step into the unknown. Until you start doing the job, you won't know whether you've made a smart move or not.

😊😊 COACHING SESSION 72

The risks of changing jobs

Here is another case study for you to consider.

Case study: Ronni

Ronni is a procurement manager with a company in the plastics industry. She has recently been for two interviews with a rival company and now they have offered her the job. Ronni is therefore at the point of having to decide whether to accept the offer or not.

Ronni's main reason for going out on the job market was money and, in this respect, the offer comes up to her expectations. What has started to play on her mind, however, is the thought of leaving a company that has practically been her second home for the past ten years and where she has made many friends. Another drawback with the rival company is that it is smaller and, as everyone in the industry has been going though tough times recently, Ronni is worried about her security. If the need for headcount cuts arose, then, as a new starter, she might be a target for redundancy.

What are your thoughts on the dilemma facing Ronni? How would you quantify the risk of changing jobs? Record your answer here.

Ronni is having more than an attack of cold feet. An inner voice is warning her that by moving jobs she could be running a risk.

The upsides and downsides

Every time you move jobs, you take a risk. However, risks always have two sides to them – the upsides and the downsides.

- **Upsides:** these are the gains you make from making the move – in Ronni's case, a better salary.

- **Downsides:** these are what happen when the job doesn't work out and you have to cope with the fall-out in terms of dealing with the damage and getting your career back on track.

Doing a risk assessment

This consists of viewing the upsides and downsides together and seeing to what extent they cancel one another out. At the same time, you also need to consider another set of risks – the ones you will be taking by turning the offer down and staying where you are. You need also to be aware that there is no such thing as the perfect job. Here, the upsides and downsides are different.

- **Upsides:** you have the comfort and security of working for an employer you know.

- **Downsides:** you continue to underachieve, stagnate, be underpaid – whatever it was that drove you on to the job market in the first place.

! COACH'S TIP

Don't change jobs for trivial reasons

Viewing the risk of moving jobs in its proper context teaches you two important lessons:

1. Never move jobs for inconsequential reasons – for example, a small increase in salary or a more impressive-sounding job title.

2. Don't change jobs to resolve minor gripes – for example, you don't like the choice of company car you've been given.

COACHING SESSION 73

A disappointing offer

Imagine that, like Ronni, you have been shopping around for a job with better pay. Finally an offer comes through but you are disappointed to see that the salary is (a) little more than you're earning now and (b) wouldn't be worth the risk of making the move. How would you deal with this situation?

Write your thoughts down here.

_____

_____

_____

_____

_____

_____

RENEGOTIATING TERMS

Some items in employers' terms are standard, so there is little point in trying to renegotiate them. One example is leave entitlement. A frequent downside of moving jobs for people who have been with the same employer for a long time is that they lose service days (the extra leave entitlement they have built up over the years). In these circumstances, trying to persuade a new employer to agree to additional leave over and above the standard entitlement may be difficult or impossible. Pay, however, may be different. Employers may have some leeway, but the only way you will discover whether they do is by testing them out.

Renegotiating pay

Where the choice is between turning an offer down and trying to renegotiate it, you are clearly losing nothing by giving it a try. Be aware, though, that seeking to renegotiate pay is a route of no return. Once you have said the salary isn't up to scratch, it is hard to go back on your words at a later stage.

When renegotiating pay, try not to give the appearance that you are negotiating. Employers tend to back off when they think someone is trying to twist their arms. Let the suggestions come from them. A model approach would be to take the following steps:

1. Act quickly and phone the person who offered you the job straight away.

2. Thank them for the offer.

3. Say that regrettably you won't be accepting and explain why. Make it clear that the salary is the *only* reason for deciding to decline. In all other respects, the offer is acceptable. There is one problem and one problem only.

4. Leave it there (don't say any more).

There are three possible outcomes here:

- **A big silence**

In this case, don't worry because you have registered the message. End the conversation. If the approach has worked, the person you have spoken to will get back to you. If there is room for renegotiation, this will tend to happen quickly.

- **A question**

You may be asked some kind of 'what if' question such as 'What if we met your figure? Would you accept then?' Be ready to say yes. Be ready to ask for the new offer in writing.

- **A negative response**

They tell you they can't increase the offer – end of story.

BAD MOVES AND HOW TO AVOID THEM

There are no two ways about it: bad moves have the potential to be catastrophic. You could end up getting the sack or quitting after the first few weeks. This means that you have to go back on the job market again and, this time, with some explaining to do.

Bad moves and why people make them frequently go back to interviews, where miscommunication – intentional or otherwise – may occur. The following checklist highlights some of the reasons for bad moves.

1. Candidates make false claims

Candidates frequently talk up how good they are, not just at interviews but also in their cover letters and CVs. Every interviewer expects you to show your best side, but if this extends to making exaggerated or false claims about your own proficiency, you are putting yourself on a dangerous path. Inexperienced interviewers may be taken in by your claims that you are the best choice for the job, to the point where you may be offered a position far beyond your capabilities. It all comes back to being yourself when you go for interviews and letting the employer judge whether or not you are up to the job.

2. The job is not the one applied for

Sometimes interviews take strange paths. You start off being interviewed for one job and end up being offered another. This happens more than most people think, and the danger here is that part of the selection process has been spent on an entirely different agenda and important areas have been missed out.

3. The job is misrepresented

Be on your guard for employers who try to sell you the job by talking only about its good points and ignoring the snags. Such employers are usually desperate and the job they are offering is the one no one will take – or not for long.

Beware, too, of employers who make big promises – for example promises of future promotions or pay increases. Be especially wary of employers who won't put their promises into writing. Beware also of employers whose answers to questions are vague or evasive. (Candidate: 'When will my pay next be reviewed?' Employer: 'We'll have to see.')

4. The job is conditional or temporary

Pick up on the kind of employers who give themselves let-outs. An example is the kind of job offer that is conditional on the retention of a contract or the business of a specified customer. Read the small print of any job offer and any supporting documentation that comes with it. Jobs sometimes have hidden catches that no one bothered to explain at any of the interviews. The hidden catch could be that the job is temporary or subject to some extended trial arrangement, which effectively means the same thing.

5. The salary is not what was quoted

With salary, watch out where the figure quoted incorporates earnings derived from performance-related elements and/or working systematic overtime. There is nothing wrong with salaries made up in this way, providing the employer is not trying to conceal something from you.

6. There is a culture clash

Watch out for culture clashes. For example, if up to now you have always worked for large professionally managed businesses with formalized structures, you could find it hard to fit into a small entrepreneurial outfit where the decisions all emanate from one person.

7. The job offer is not as expected

Be on your guard when you think you are being made an offer you can't refuse (there will be more on this next). Spot, too, where there are variances between what employers say at interviews and what they put in their job offers.

COACHING SESSION 74

Add your own tips for avoiding a bad move

Having read the checklist above, think about what you have learned from your own experience of making bad moves (what lessons you can pass on to others). Use the space below to add your own tips to those in the checklist.

_____

_____

_____

_____

_____

_____

_____

_____

> ## ! COACH'S TIP
>
> ### Listen to your inner voices
>
> When you are locked in negotiations with employers, listen to your inner voices and take note of what they're telling you – they rarely let you down.

THE PERILS OF ENTICEMENT

The enticement of sought-after people from one employer to another has turned into a major industry. Yet succumbing to enticement (accepting an offer you can't refuse) is one of the commonest reasons why people make bad moves. Enticement can come in a number of forms – not just in terms of salary but also in the perks, impressive-sounding job titles and, increasingly today, big upfront payments, or 'golden hellos'.

While, on the face of it, negotiating a package with mouth-watering items such as these may make you feel that you have landed the job of your dreams, it could also mean that the employer you are in negotiation with is in dire straits and knows of no other way of getting you to take the job. Gut instinct will often tell you how far you can trust people, and you will need to pay attention to this where your knowledge of the people in question is confined to what you have learned over the course of two or three interviews.

> ## ! COACH'S TIP
>
> ### Trust your gut instinct
>
> A job with a fat-cat salary and a big flash car will do you no good at all if it lasts only six months. Gut instinct is a natural warning device, an accumulation of all the lessons you have learned in life, and it is interesting to note how many times people who have made bad moves say afterwards, 'I knew I was making a mistake, but…'

RESPONDING TO OFFERS OF EMPLOYMENT

Once you have a job offer, it is a good idea to phone the person who made the offer on the same day as you receive it. The purpose of the phone call is to say thank you for the offer and give a response. This might be an immediate yes, or it might be to say that you now need a few days to consider it carefully (big decision etc.). As another example of keeping control, you need to indicate when you will be able to confirm your decision.

COACHING SESSION 75

Deciding whether to accept

Here is another case study illustrating the experience of someone on the job market in search of more money.

Case study: Tess

Tess is delighted to receive a job offer giving her a 20-per-cent improvement on her current salary. She has every intention of accepting it. With this in mind, she arranges a meeting with her boss, Jason. As she sees it, the purpose of this meeting is to tell Jason what she has been offered and to hand in her notice.

Jason, however, is shocked when he hears her news and asks Tess whether she is prepared to change her mind if he can persuade the Managing Director to match the offer. Caught off guard, Tess says yes and Jason promises to get back to her as soon as possible.

A week goes by with no word from Jason so Tess catches him one night as he is leaving the office. Jason, she senses, is unhappy to see her and soon she finds out why. He has seen the MD, who has said that the best the company can offer her to stay is a 10-per-cent increase now and the promise of a review later in the year. Tess says that she is disappointed and writes her notice out there and then.

When Tess gets home she puts together a letter accepting the offer and giving a date on which she can start. However, two days later she gets an email back from the company who made her the offer saying that, as they hadn't heard from her, they have offered the job to someone else.

1. What are your thoughts on Tess's situation?

_____

_____

_____

_____

_____

2. What did she do wrong and what could she have done better?

_____

_____

_____

_____

_____

In fairness to Tess, she can't be accused of using the offer to secure a pay rise for herself. That suggestion came from her boss. But where she did fall down was in her failure to communicate with her prospective employer. Because they didn't hear from her, they took the view that Tess wasn't interested in what they had to offer and, like many employers, they have got used to people who don't have the decency to respond. While some employers would have fired off a warning shot – a letter or an email to Tess giving her a deadline for her response and telling her that after a certain date the offer would be withdrawn – there is no guarantee that employers in a hurry to fill vacancies will go to such lengths.

Leaving voids in the way that Tess did is simply inviting trouble. Given that she was waiting to hear from Jason on the outcome of his discussion with the MD, she should have been aware of the following:

1. It doesn't take weeks to think over job offers – an indication to the new employers of how long she needed to decide would have been sensible.

2. Employers have had problems with people who use their job offers just to get themselves a pay rise.

3. The same timescale should have been extended to her boss Jason so that everyone knew where they stood.

All of the above is yet another example of the importance of keeping control. All Tess can do now is ask Jason whether she can withdraw her notice – not a satisfactory outcome for her.

! COACH'S TIP

Don't delay your decision

Employers won't wait indefinitely for people to give their response to a job offer. They give them so long and then move on.

→ NEXT STEPS

After getting through the interviews, being told that you have got the job should be a moment of elation. However, this is where you must face the reality of your position. Is it time to hand in your notice or is something telling you to think twice?

Putting in a brilliant interview performance has no purpose if you don't land a good job at the end of it. If you find that you are repeatedly getting into situations where you can't make your mind up about offers put in front of you, you need to address this. If you don't, you could find yourself automatically reverting to a default position every time – in this case, turning offers down.

In this chapter you have learned to make the important distinction between:

- offers of employment you are right to reject
- those where you can't make your mind up.

You have learned to carry out a proper risk assessment before making your decision, remembering that there is no such thing as the perfect job. There will be upsides and downsides to every offer you receive and there is always the risk that, due to some factor that neither you nor the employer has considered, the job still doesn't work out. In short, there is always a risk to taking a new job and hence the advice only to take on the risk if the upsides are sufficiently good. This balancing of the risks is all part of mastering the art of interviews.

The next chapter looks at:

- what you can learn from the experience of going to interviews
- how you can use the experience and build on it.

👍 TAKEAWAYS

When it comes to knowing whether to accept a job that has been offered to you or whether to turn it down, have you ever been faced by indecisiveness? Do you think that the section in this chapter on carrying out a proper risk assessment will help you if you ever find yourself in this position again? Make a note here of anything you found particularly helpful.

_____

_____

_____

_____

_____

_____

_____

_____

_____

As a result of reading this chapter, would you feel more confident if you were ever put in the position of having to renegotiate the terms in a job offer? What would you do now that you would not have thought to do previously?

_____

_____

_____

_____

_____

_____

_____

_____

_____

Has reading this chapter taught you anything new about what you can do to avoid making bad moves? List here any points that you picked out.

_____

_____

_____

_____

_____

_____

_____

_____

Have you ever felt you were being made an offer you couldn't refuse? Based on what you have learned in this chapter, would you act differently if you found yourself in the same position again? Say in what ways.

_____

_____

_____

_____

_____

_____

_____

_____

_____

Has the section on responding to offers of employment taught you anything you didn't know before? What have you learned and is it something that you will find useful?

_____

_____

_____

_____

_____

_____

_____

_____

_____

_____

_____

_____

_____

_____

_____

_____

_____

11 | MOVING YOUR INTERVIEWS FORWARD

✔ OUTCOMES FROM THIS CHAPTER

- Recognize the dangers of negative thinking.
- Learn how to build on experience.
- Understand the importance of seeing every interview as a fresh challenge.

THE DANGERS OF NEGATIVE THINKING

One of the big dangers of negative thinking is that it is a state of mind that is difficult to escape from. It taints everything and eventually turns into cynicism of the kind that doesn't help when you are trying to stay focused on achieving an aim. The only remedy in some cases is to take a break from job-hunting and go back to it when the negative thoughts have disappeared.

🗩🗩 COACHING SESSION 76

The state of negative thinking

Consider this case study. It brings in some of the lessons from previous chapters.

Case study: Phil

Phil has spent a lifetime in the distribution industry, first as a warehouse supervisor then, more recently, in management roles. He is now 48 and his current position is Operations Manager in charge of six distribution centres employing around 350 people.

Phil still considers himself to be ambitious and for some time he has been looking for an opportunity to step up the ladder into a top management job. So far, however, his experience has not been good. Over the last two years he has applied for more jobs than he can remember and been to dozens of interviews – in some cases being asked to go back three or four times. To date, however, he has had no job offers and he is now starting to think that his lack of success is either because he is seen as too old or because he has come up the hard way (he hasn't been to university or got a degree).

Phil has begun to resign himself to the fact that his career may have peaked. He can't do anything about his age and taking the time out to study for qualifications is impractical for someone like him, with a family to support and bills to pay. As far as applying for more jobs is concerned, Phil is starting to think 'What's the point?'

What are your thoughts on this case study? Answer these questions:

1. How would you rate Phil's interview performance?

_____

_____

_____

_____

_____

2. Could he be right about the reasons he has come up with for his lack of success?

_____

_____

_____

_____

_____

3. If he keeps going with his applications, how do you rate his chances of success from here on?

_____

_____

_____

_____

_____

4. What advice would you give him?

_____

_____

_____

_____

_____

As Phil's case study shows, people whose heads are full of negativity start thinking the world is against them. They feel that they are banging their heads against a brick wall or locked in a battle they can't win. Phil is typical of people who have no real idea about why more of their interviews don't turn into jobs. They fill the space by taking false readings of the situation and substituting their own interpretations.

Doing a reality check

The problem for Phil is that he has entered into a state of negative thinking which has clouded his sense of reality. He is now ready to give up. To keep going would be difficult for him. To coin his own phrase: 'What's the point?'

In reality, Phil has had success in getting interviews and some of these interviews have resulted in him being asked to go back for further interviews. This tells you that he has come very close to getting some of the jobs and, in the context of the jobs he is applying for (top jobs), his performance is clearly not as poor as he thinks. In fact, he has done well and, if he can manage to keep going, he will, sooner or later, land one of the jobs.

While anything is possible, it seems highly unlikely that Phil is correct in his belief that no one seems interested in him because he is seen as under-qualified or too old. The information about his age and qualifications could have been deduced from reading his CV and, if these facts were an issue for the employers concerned, a far easier option would have been to leave him off the interview list.

Putting it down to experience

It is only natural to ask questions when the outcome of an interview isn't the one you wanted. Did you do anything wrong? Is there anything you can learn from the experience and put right next time?

Because, as we have seen, getting helpful feedback after an interview is almost impossible, it is easy to understand why people like Phil insert their own interpretations and, like Phil, usually end up stabbing in the dark. However, agonizing over what went wrong at an interview is largely wasted effort. You would be better off spending your time doing the next application.

BAD INTERVIEW EXPERIENCES

Being kept waiting or being interviewed by people who don't appear to know what they are doing – these are the kinds of experiences that sometimes cause candidates to have second thoughts about pursuing their applications any further.

⚏ COACHING SESSION 77

The bad interview experience

The next case study looks at how bad interview experiences can affect people.

Case study: Shah

Shah is in his early thirties and currently employed as a teacher. He wants to use his engineering degree to make a move into the field of design of hydraulic and pneumatic systems, a field that has always interested him.

Shah has been applying for jobs for the last six months and getting nowhere until a letter arrives in the post inviting him to an interview with the technical manager of one of the major players in the industry. Shah is very pleased to get the interview and gives a lot of thought to preparing himself.

On the day he arrives on time, only to be kept waiting in a reception area for nearly an hour. Finally, a woman appears who tells him that the interviewer has been called to a meeting and the interview will have to be rearranged. Shah asks the woman when he should come back, to which she replies that she does not know – she is just passing on a message.

On his journey home, Shah reflects on his experience. The woman did not apologize at any point, which strikes Shah as bad manners. During his one-hour wait, no one bothered to explain what was happening. No one thought to ask him if he wanted a drink – further evidence in Shah's view that, despite its impressive reputation, the company is not one he would want to work for, even if a job were offered to him. Whether he will ever hear from the company again is an open question but, if he does and is offered another interview, Shah decides he will decline.

1. What would you do in Shah's position?

_____

_____

_____

_____

_____

2. Given his experience, would you strike the company off your list of prospective employers?

_____

_____

_____

_____

_____

Bad interview experiences are commonplace and for a variety of reasons, ranging from interviewers who talk too much through to the kind of treatment Shah received. But pause for thought. Interviewers who make a hash of their interviews aren't necessarily bad people to work for, and busy managers do get called into meetings at short notice. When the summons comes from someone at the top of the tree, the same managers are not always in a position to say, 'Sorry, I've got someone in reception waiting to be interviewed.'

A better job could have been made of explaining to Shah what was happening, but, when crises erupt in organizations, such niceties can and do get overlooked. Of course, a far better approach would have been for the interviewer to have spoken to Shah himself rather than leave it to a messenger who didn't seem to have many interpersonal skills, but that's life. That's the way it goes sometimes.

> ## ! COACH'S TIP
>
> **Don't let bad interview experiences put you off**
>
> If an interviewer is shifty and evasive, that is a different matter, but if they are simply inexperienced it would be a mistake to judge them or the organizations they represent on this basis alone.

SEEING EVERY INTERVIEW AS A FRESH CHALLENGE

This is the corollary to not allowing your actions to be tainted by negative thinking: go into every interview with a fresh mind. You will be meeting different people with their own ideas – ideas that won't be the same as the ideas of the last set of people you met. You go in again and give it your best shot. This time it could be you who gets the job.

COACHING SESSION 78

How you have improved

Has your experience of going to interviews made you better at them? Go through the following list of qualities and put a tick alongside those where you think your performance has improved as a result of your experience. Add anything else you have improved on to the list.

I'm...	✓ / ✗
• better at making a good impression on interviewers	
• more confident about the outcome	
• better at being myself	
• less nervous before an interview	
• better at answering questions	
• better at spotting when the interviewer hasn't asked the right questions	
• better at knowing what to do about it	
• better at ending interviews on a positive note	
• better at knowing what questions I should be asking	
•	
•	

BUILDING ON THE GOOD

The list above shows some of the lessons you can carry forward from one interview to the next. In this way, you will be building on the good rather than carrying forward negative thoughts (thoughts you would be better off leaving in the past, where they belong).

To summarize the learning you will have taken from this book, here is a list of key points gathered together from the other chapters.

- An interview is about presenting yourself to an employer in a way that accurately reflects who you are and what you can do.

- Conversely, an interview is not about presenting yourself as someone you are not.

- Don't see employers as the enemy or try to pull the wool over their eyes. They have as much interest in getting it right as you do. Try to help them make the right decision.

- Learn to live with the diversity of interviews – the good and the bad. Don't pollute your mind with negative thoughts. Surviving and winning in today's world of interviews means handling whatever comes your way and taking it in your stride.

- Don't see interviews as a stand-alone process. They are important but they are just a step on the journey from applying for a job to walking away with the offer in your hand. Being brilliant at interviews isn't an end in itself.

- Don't view interview success in terms of the number of jobs you are offered. The jobs you get need to be the right ones.

- You won't get the job every time, so don't expect to, but don't let this get in the way of going for the next one.

→ NEXT STEPS

In this final chapter, you have been looking at how you can build on the experience of going to interviews and become better at them. Here, it is important to be selective about what you take forward – to forget the negative and focus on the good. Where there are large numbers of applicants for a job, getting an interview is a major feat in itself and a sign that you have done everything right so far. Getting on the shortlist shows that you are close to getting the job. However, if it doesn't work out, shrug it off and move on to the next application. Sooner or later, you will get there.

Don't do what a lot of candidates do and start agonizing over what went wrong and then spend countless hours redesigning CVs or rehearsing strange interview techniques. Instead, take the view that there is a job waiting for you somewhere out there and, providing you keep going, you will find it.

👍 TAKEAWAYS

Has your experience of interviews caused you to lapse into negative thinking? After reading this chapter, what do you plan to do about it?

_____

_____

_____

_____

_____

_____

_____

_____

_____

_____

_____

_____

_____

As a result of reading this chapter, have you changed your ideas about what constitutes success when it comes to interviews? If your ideas have changed, say in what way.

_____

_____

_____

_____

_____

_____

_____

_____

_____

_____

_____

_____

_____

Have you had any further thoughts on not letting bad interview experiences put you off? Did any examples come to mind of where an interviewer's poor performance affected you in this way? How did you react at the time? Would you react in the same way now?

_____

_____

_____

_____

_____

_____

_____

_____

_____

Did the section on building on the good make you pause for thought? After reading this section, did anything come to mind that you could relate to your own experience?

_____

_____

_____

_____

_____

_____

_____

_____

_____

Did you check out the online resource ('Are you an interviewer's nightmare?')? Did anything in the article make you think? Make a note of any points that struck you and could flag up the need for you to take corrective action.

_____

_____

_____

_____

_____

_____

_____

_____

_____

_____

_____

_____

_____

_____

_____

_____

_____

_____

_____

_____

_____

_____

ONLINE RESOURCE

Are you an interviewer's nightmare?

Often, candidates have only themselves to blame for interviews not covering all the ground they need to cover or running out of time. Access the free download to find out what you need to do to avoid your interviewers tearing their hair out with frustration. Go to the following website:

www.TYCoachbooks.com/Interviews

HELP DESK

INTERVIEW NERVES

'What do interviewers make of people who suffer from interview nerves? Does it suggest that they are lacking in confidence and, if so, would it be seen as a bad sign?'

Interview nerves are natural (most people suffer from them), so a candidate who spends the first few minutes of an interview looking ill at ease won't be seen as out of the ordinary. On the other hand, a candidate who walks into the room exuding confidence from every pore might be seen as putting on an act. So the message on interview nerves is to forget them. In any case, they tend to wear off as soon as the interview gets into its stride.

GOING FOR AN INTERVIEW AND HEARING NOTHING

'I went for an interview and then heard nothing – no letter, no email, no phone call to let me know whether I'd got the job or not. Is this experience typical?'

It may not be typical but there are certainly employers out there who behave in the way you describe. While we are not offering excuses for anyone, the reason in many cases is managers with too much on their plates putting the job of informing unsuccessful candidates to one side, then finding that they don't get round to it. Like all bad interview experiences, the best advice to you is to forget it.

OFFERS OF EMPLOYMENT: A BETTER JOB IN THE PIPELINE

'I was shortlisted for two jobs – Job A and Job B. Job B is better than Job A, both in terms of the salary and the long-term prospects. I have been offered Job A and the employer concerned is now pressing me for an answer. I have phoned the Job B employer to explain my predicament, only to be told that they won't be able to let me have a decision for at least two weeks. I honestly don't feel I can keep Job A open much longer and certainly not for two weeks. What do I do?'

Take Job A. If Job B then comes through, take it, then write to the Job A employer and say that you've changed your mind because you've had another offer. The job market is not a tidy place, so you will rarely, if ever, be in a position where all the jobs you are offered arrive at the same time or in the order you would like.

OFFERS OF EMPLOYMENT: NOT AS EXPECTED FROM THE INTERVIEW

'At an interview I attended recently, a salary was quoted that was higher than I expected. However, when the job offer came through, a lower figure was quoted. Everything else in the offer was fine but I don't know what to do about the salary. Should I query it?'

There's certainly no harm in querying it but it sounds as if the interviewer got it wrong – something that happens more often than you might think. If, as we suspect, the salary in the offer is the right one, then you need to go back to your original idea about what it would take to make it worth while for you to move. If the salary in the offer meets your aspirations, then take the job.

UNEXPECTED TERMS IN A JOB OFFER

'I received a job offer recently with a clause preventing me from working for a competitor for a period of six months after leaving. While I understand the reasons for these restraint clauses, particularly in management contracts, I am concerned because (a) nothing was said about the clause at any of the interviews I attended and (b) what happens if they make me redundant? My concern with (b) is that I have spent all my working life in one trade, so taking competitors out of the frame would make me practically unemployable.'

There is probably nothing sinister about the fact that the restraint clause wasn't mentioned at the interviews. As you say, they are fairly standard items in management contracts. With regard to redundancy, read the small print carefully to see whether your concerns are answered in the shape of a waiver covering enforced redundancy. If you don't come across anything, go back to the employer, tell them what your worries are and ask them to put something in writing to say the restraint would not apply if, apart from misconduct, termination of your employment was not out of choice.

FEEDBACK FOLLOWING AN INTERVIEW

'I recently attended an interview arranged for me by an agency. I didn't get the job and I asked the agency to see whether they could get any feedback from the employer on why I hadn't been successful. The feedback, when it came, was that the interviewer felt that I lacked ambition, though it wasn't explained how she had arrived at this conclusion. Can you suggest what I can do to come across as more ambitious so that I'll do better at my next interview?'

Never act on the feedback from one interview because it is no more than one person's opinion and the next person to interview you might see you entirely differently. The advice for when you go to the next interview would be to carry on being yourself – don't, whatever you do, try to affect a more ambitious personality because it will come across as false.

TRAVELLING EXPENSES

'I have been invited to go for an interview a long way from where I live. In the letter inviting me to the interview, there is no mention of the employer paying travelling expenses, which concerns me because I am in a low-paid job and consequently hard up. My plan is to raise the subject of reimbursement when I get to the interview and see what response I get. What do you think of this idea?'

Let's say the employer is one of the many who take the view that meeting the cost of getting to an interview is the candidate's problem, not theirs. If so, asking the interviewer for reimbursement is going to be greeted by a 'no' – so the interview will have got off to a bad start. Remember what this book says about the first few minutes of an interview being important (when the first impressions form). A better way of enquiring about travelling expenses is to phone up and ask them *before* you go to the interview.

INTERVIEW MIX-UP

'I recently had the strange experience of going for an interview then, when I got there, being told that I'd come on the wrong day. The interviewer insisted that she was right and, realizing that there was no point in arguing, I said I would come back on the date when, according to her, I should have attended in the first place. However, what upsets me most is that this mistake on the interviewer's part made me look disorganized, which I am not. I did have high hopes of getting this job. Any advice?'

Mix-ups over interview times and dates happen more frequently than you might think. Someone had the wrong page of their diary open when they fixed the interview, which is why it's always advisable to have something in writing. As you say, you have potentially scored a bad first impression and recovery won't be easy, although not impossible. The best thing to do is to go along, give an excellent interview and hope for the best. Who knows, with a bit of luck the interviewer's long-term memory may be no better than her diary management.

SMART ANSWERS TO TRICKY QUESTIONS

'You don't seem to think much of the idea of having a list of smart answers to tricky questions up your sleeve when you go for an interview. Is this correct and, if so, why?'

The time that candidates often put into rehearsing these so-called smart answers would be better spent on basics such as revisiting their cover letters and CVs. Interviewers have probably heard all these smart answers before, so (a) they won't be impressed and (b) they could start to see you as someone who is putting on an act, so your credibility suffers.

ACTION PLAN

1. What five main things in the book surprised you?

1 _____

_____

2 _____

_____

3 _____

_____

4 _____

_____

5 _____

_____

2. What will you keep doing, do more of, and do less of in the future?

Tomorrow	This week	This month	This year

3. Make a list of three new SMART goals that you are going to take on as a result of having read the book.

Goal	Specific?	Measurable?	Achievable?	Relevant?	Time-bound?
1					
2					
3					

4. Use this space to write in your action plan for the next time you go to an interview.

_____

_____

_____

_____

_____

_____

_____

_____

_____

_____

_____

_____

_____

_____

_____

_____

_____

_____

_____

_____

! COACHING SESSION 79

Revisit Coaching session 1

Go back to the test at the end of the Introduction and do it again. Take note of any of the questions where your answers have changed after reading the book.

QUICK HELP

Here are the key ideas from the book, to use as an aide-memoire.

INTRODUCTION

Interviews come in all shapes and sizes and are inherently unpredictable.

Think about your attitude towards interviews.

1 THE POWER OF YOU

Understand the importance of being yourself when you go to an interview.

Know how to be better at engaging with employers.

See the value of making a good first impression.

Examine the quality of the image you present to people you've never met before.

Understand the importance of credibility.

2 PUTTING YOURSELF ON THE MARKET

Know what you need to consider before you start applying for jobs.

Treat the time you can take off work to go to interviews as (a) precious and (b) not to be squandered.

Avoid interviews that are time-wasters.

Take away barriers that you might be putting in the way of employers who want to talk to you.

Think carefully about how you respond to employers' emails and phone calls.

3 HANDLING THE DIVERSITY OF INTERVIEWS

Understand the difference between good and bad interviews.

Understand different types of interview and what to expect.

Plan strategies for interviews to take account of their diversity.

Understand the importance of managing interviews and keeping control.

Know how to spot where the problem could be you.

4 WHAT TO DO BEFORE AN INTERVIEW

Know what you need to do before you go for an interview.

Understand how to research employers so you know more about what to expect.

Think about the important messages you need to get across (the messages that will enhance your chances of getting the job).

Know what questions you need to ask.

5 INTERVIEW QUESTIONS

Learn how to handle the questions that interviewers ask.

Understand what's behind the questions.

Know how to deal with the questions that interviewers don't ask.

6 PRELIMINARY INTERVIEWS

Identify the challenges you face when you go for a preliminary interview.

Know what to take with you.

Understand what to do when it's your turn to ask questions.

Know how to close the interview.

7 ON THE SHORTLIST

Understand what it means to be on a shortlist.

Identify the different challenges you face.

Recognize the importance of not relaxing your efforts.

Know what factors influence employers when it comes to making final decisions.

8 INTERVIEWS THROUGH PROACTIVE SOURCING

Know about the invisible job market and what defines it.

Understand what proactive sourcing means.

Understand how interviews for jobs sourced proactively differ from those for jobs sourced by other means.

Know what challenges you face when you go for an interview that has been sourced proactively and how to deal with them.

9 AFTER INTERVIEWS

After an interview, know how to rate your chances of success.

Know what to read into it when you're not offered the job.

Understand the importance of not doing anything that might spoil your chances of success.

10 GETTING THE JOB

Know how to approach the decision about whether to accept an offer.

Understand how to consider the risks.

Know what to do when a job offer falls short of your expectations.

Recognize a bad move and know how to avoid making one.

Know what to do when you've made up your mind to accept an offer.

11 MOVING YOUR INTERVIEWS FORWARD

Recognize the dangers of negative thinking.

Know how to build on experience.

Understand the importance of seeing every interview as a fresh challenge.

INDEX